CONFLICT

CONFLICT

*African American Women
and the New Dilemma
of Race and Gender Politics*

Cindy Hooper

 PRAEGER

AN IMPRINT OF ABC-CLIO, LLC
Santa Barbara, California • Denver, Colorado • Oxford, England

Library of Congress Cataloging-in-Publication Data

Hooper, Cindy,
  Conflict : African American women and the new dilemma of race and gender politics / Cindy Hooper.
       p. cm.
  Includes bibliographical references and index.
  ISBN 978-0-313-39214-6 (hardcopy : alk. paper) — ISBN 978-0-313-39215-3 (ebook)
  1. African American women—Political activity—History—20th century.   2. African American women—Political activity—History—21st century.   3. African American feminists—Political activity—History—20th century.   4. African American feminists—Political activity—History—21st century.   5. African American women—Race identity.   6. United States—Race relations.   I. Title.
  E185.86.H744   2012
  305.48896073—dc23   2012017550

ISBN: 978-0-313-39214-6
EISBN: 978-0-313-39215-3

16   15   14   13   12   2   3   4   5

This book is also available on the World Wide Web as an eBook.
Visit www.abc-clio.com for details.

Praeger
An Imprint of ABC-CLIO, LLC

ABC-CLIO, LLC
130 Cremona Drive, P.O. Box 1911
Santa Barbara, California 93116-1911

This book is printed on acid-free paper ∞

Manufactured in the United States of America

Contents

Introduction

Black men decry racism, women decry sexism, Black women decry half as much despite being hit twice as hard.

—Cindy Hooper

Today, African American women can stand proudly on the legacy of millions of humanists: men, women, and even children of various races and ethnicities who laid the groundwork for the world that many have the opportunity to thrive in today. Grateful for the sacrifices and the trailblazing that would have prevented any of us in this current day from living the exuberant lives that are led in this new millennium, we pay homage to the indebtedness of so many throughout our history.

The new millennium Black woman has vast amounts of opportunity that her forbearers could only imagine. Black women are the chief executive officers of Fortune 500 companies, mayors of major cities, Nobel Prize winners, Olympic gold medalists, and now a Black woman stands tall as the first lady of the United States. The world has changed dramatically since the first Africans were brought to the shores of America. There are Black women in positions of power and influence that their ancestors could only dream of.

For the first time in history, the first lady of the United States is an African American woman. Oprah Winfrey, media mogul and one of the most influential and wealthiest people on the planet, is an African American woman. African American women are now in power positions to influence not only the nation, but also the world.

When *Forbes* announced the 25 power women of the 2010 midterm elections, Michelle Obama was the only African American woman on the list. She campaigned for numerous Democratic Party candidates during the midterm election season including in key battleground states. In some cases, she became a bigger draw on the campaign trail than the president, hosting events that outsold other events hosted by her president husband.

The new millennium Black woman has definitely arrived to embrace a new diaspora. Being socialized in a patriarchal society, the selfless humanity of the African American woman has her routinely putting everyone else's priorities above hers. It is difficult to decipher the fact that the African American woman—an African and American cultural treasure—is the least partnered group in the nation.

Black women have had to maneuver between both their racial and gender identities for centuries within the legal and political landscape, since the American legal system both perpetuated and sanctioned racism and sexism. The tumultuous journey began as early as 1641 when Massachusetts made slavery legal, declaring that a child inherited its free or slave status from the mother. In 1662, the Virginia House of Burgesses declared that a child's slave status followed the mother's—*if the mother was not White.*

In 1668, Virginia declared that Black women should pay taxes, *but not White women*—whether they were free or not. In 1780, Massachusetts abolished slavery and gave Black men, not Black women, the right to vote. In later decades, Black female abolitionists and women's rights advocates would lobby hard for the passage of both the Fourteenth and Fifteenth Amendments, even though neither Amendment gave the right to vote to women.

In 1919, the first chair of the National Association for the Advancement of Colored People (NAACP) was Mary White Ovington, a White woman. Ovington incidentally was also a suffragette. Fifty-six years later, Mary Bush Wilson became the first Black female board chair of the NAACP in 1975.

Even though women in the United States were granted the right to vote in 1920 by the Nineteenth Amendment to the Constitution, many Black women were disenfranchised and prevented from voting by legal and other means. These means included but were not limited to the infamous literacy tests and poll taxes. Many Black women would have to wait until the passage of the Voting Rights Act decades later to fully enfranchise their voting rights.

There were numerous instances where White women supported the fight for the dignity and inherent rights of Black women. One of the most noted was the resignation of first lady Eleanor Roosevelt from the Daughters of the American Revolution (DAR) when Marian Anderson was denied the opportunity to perform at DAR's Constitution Hall in 1939 because of her race.

In 1968, Black women took their first monumental step into elective office on the federal level when the Honorable Shirley Chisholm was elected to the U.S. House of Representatives. Since that time, 31 African American women have served in the U.S. Congress.

Today's millennium Black woman has to do it all: cook, clean, work, nurture, and raise children oftentimes alone. History has had a difficult time in giving full light to the true contributions of Black women. Descendants of the African diaspora, including African American women, have had a tremendous impact on American history.

African American women were ostracized and marginalized during the women's suffrage movement. As far back as 1832, a group of Black women in Massachusetts created the first women's antislavery society in America. In 1834, it expanded the organization to include White women. The American Equal Rights Association was organized in 1866 to address both women's issues and Black rights. In 1868, activists within the American Equal Rights Association split over which group should take priority focus of the organization's focus: Black men or Black women.

There were still Black suffragists, such as Frances Ellen Watkins Harper who sided with Black men to ensure the passing of the Fifteenth Amendment, to the chagrin of many within the suffrage movement. During the civil rights movement, Black women stepped aside as Black men took the visible leadership roles. Many feminists also had instrumental roles in the civil rights movement. Black women were an afterthought in both movements.

Many Black women even today believe that feminism is primarily a White middle class construct. The oftentimes differing realities of Black women and members of the feminist movement create a rift between the parties involved. There are women, however, who fought fervently for both racial and gender equality such as Jean Downey and the renowned Pauli Murray. Murray was one of a number of prominent Black women who were both civil rights activists and prominent leaders of the feminist movement. Murray was also one of the African American founders of the National Organization for Women in addition to Shirley Chisholm, the first African American woman to run for president of the United States in 1972.

Racism is deeply embedded in the history of African American culture. At times, Black women have often been accused of misguided racial loyalty at the expense of their gender priorities. African American women have throughout history fought the multiple oppressions of being female, Black, and oftentimes economically disadvantaged. While "White Only" signs are no longer visible in the United States and discriminatory hiring practices have somewhat diminished, even today, African American women must continue to fight racism and sexism simultaneously. It is an ongoing unfortunate fact of life for so many. Despite that, African American women continue the fight for social, economic, and political empowerment for all involved.

Conflict: African American Women and the New Dilemma of Race and Gender Politics examines the development of a voting bloc of women within the national political landscape. There is a significant underrepresentation of women in elective office in proportion to their percentage of the U.S. population. This book reveals astonishing data to indicate an even greater underrepresentation for African American women and the impact that it has on the political and social empowerment of women of color.

For the first time in U.S. history, a woman and an African American man competed for the nomination of a major political party for the office of the presidency of the United States. This question has been asked time and again: Would African American women support the African American candidate or the female candidate in this critical 2008 presidential election? What would be the basis of their decision? Would it be identity politics or a close examination of the candidates' positions on issues of relevance?

African American women have struggled for decades to find their place in American politics. This book reviews the historical perspective of African American women and their roles in both the women's suffrage and civil rights movements. The racial bias experienced within the women's suffrage movement and the gender bias experienced within the civil rights movement kept African American women on a continual quest to seek their own distinct place in American politics.

Both movements essentially failed to adequately address the specific needs of Black women, and a form of Black feminism emerged. Black feminism was the feminist ideology that gave light to the unique history of the racial and gender oppression of Black women. This book looks at how the eventual failure of Black feminism made Black women transfer their ambitions back to the ballot box. From this, Shirley Chisholm and Carol Moseley Braun emerged as trailblazers for Black women in politics.

Chapter 1 includes a detailed review of the statistics indicating the underrepresentation of women in elective office in the United States. Included is the overwhelming evidence of an even greater underrepresentation of African American women in elective office. Chapter 2 examines the progression of women in elective office in the United States from a historical perspective. This includes a detailed review of the legacy of African American female pioneers in politics, such as Shirley Chisholm and Carol Moseley Braun.

Further along into the book, in chapter 3, the effect of the early political mobilization of African American women is reviewed and how this mobilization helped to shape African American women's views on gender identity. The discrimination faced by African American women within the suffrage movement is also examined. The effect of the omission of African American women from public leadership roles in the civil rights movement is critically analyzed in chapter 4. This chapter also looks at the major roles that these women had in the background of the movement.

Chapter 5 examines the failure of Black feminism in adequately addressing the specific needs of African American women. Included in this chapter is a look into Black feminist ideology that grew out of the unique history of the racial and gender oppression of Black women. For the first time in the U.S. history, a woman and an African American man ran for the nomination of a major party for the presidential nomination. Chapter 6 looks at what the election of either will mean for the advancement of African American women politically, economically, and socially.

As late as November 2007, at least 60 percent of African American women polled were supporting the candidacy of Hillary Clinton for president of the United States. Chapter 7 examines why the support from the African American female demographic was so fervent for Senator Clinton, including a look at the influence of the legacy of former president Bill Clinton. African American women's support for presidential candidate Barack Obama gave him critical primary victories in numerous states, including North and South Carolina, in effect making him the Democratic frontrunner. Chapter 8 examines the catalysts responsible for this important shift, including the impact of Oprah Winfrey.

Chapter 9 provides an intriguing examination of African American women's impact in the recent presidential elections in the years 2000 and 2004 and how that impact gives us a preview of the possibilities for the presidential election of 2008. The focus of chapter 10 is on the key primaries of the 2008 presidential campaign where the impact of the record participation of African Americans and African American women, in particular, tilted the vote in favor of presidential candidate, Barack Obama. Could the direct impact of African American women voters elect our next president?

African American women have remarked that they feel a deep sense of obligation in electing either the first female president or the first African American president. Which side do African American women feel a stronger sense of loyalty to, their gender or their race? Chapter 11 analyzes the premise that this phenomenon may be changing as a result of this year's presidential race. The content of chapter 12 offers a provocative examination of how this emerging voting bloc is no longer being ignored as it has in decades past and what the implications are as this demographic emerges as a legitimate power player within the political landscape.

The question has been asked time and again: Were African American women going to support the African American candidate or the female candidate in this unique 2008 presidential election? Time and again the responses were inconclusive. Where do African American women stand on the issues relevant to them? This book ponders which side African American women identify with more, their gender or their race. The reality may well be that this dual identity group will select candidates who they feel will represent their views and positions on contemporary issues that affect their overall quality of life.

Conflict: African American Women and the New Dilemma of Race and Gender Politics offers a provocative examination of how this emerging dual identity group is no longer being overlooked. African American women represent the majority of the African American electorate. By providing data on voting trends from the 2008 presidential primary season and others, this book delivers the undeniable proof that African American women by supporting Senator Barack Obama in key states such as North Carolina, Georgia, Mississippi, and South Carolina, which established Obama as the Democratic frontrunner, may have a direct effect in electing the next president of the United States.

This volume explores all of the above events. It takes a look at what it has meant to be female and Black throughout America's history. Black women have sometimes been torn. Conflicts have arisen over time due to the multiple aspects of Black women's identities, but Black women have become a powerful minority in their own right, paving new roads and affecting voting patterns and life in America. The new millennium Black woman of today owes much to her previous generations and has much of which she can be proud.

Many have asked: *I beg the question, what are you? Are you a woman first or are you Black first?* For many, the answer is simple: *I am proud to be gifted, female, AND Black.*

Chapter 1

Cohesive Representation

Of my two "handicaps," being female put more obstacles in my path than being black.

—Shirley Chisholm

Despite the implied promises of the passing of the historic Nineteenth Amendment in the year 1920, women in the United States still face underrepresentation in national, state, and local politics. Throughout history women have influenced the policies of this nation through community activism, mobilization, and elective office. As of 2010, women made up approximately 20 percent of the total number of officials in elective office, despite women representing almost half of the population in the United States of America.[1]

We are making strides when it comes to electing women to positions of power in this country. In 2010, there were 90 representatives that are women in the U.S. Congress. Of the 100 members of the U.S. Senate, 17 were women. There were 73 women in the U.S. House of Representatives representing 31 different states. Currently, 24.5 percent of the state legislators in the United States are women, and of the 254 mayors of U.S. cities with populations over 100,000, 17.5 percent are women.[2]

It was a huge step forward for women in the political arena when, in 2007, U.S. Congresswoman Nancy Pelosi became the Speaker of the House of Representatives. Pelosi was the highest-ranking female government official in the history of the United States. As Speaker of the House, she was second in line in the succession to the presidency of the United States.

African American women are in a unique position. Since the year 1619 when a Dutch ship brought 20 enslaved Africans to Jamestown, Virginia,[3]

African American women have been hostages in the tridimensional conflicts of racism, sexism, and classism. Their history is distinct, mired with episodes of forced servitude and racial oppression. One could strongly argue that no other dual identity group in the world has had the experience of the African American woman. We are as a nation living the historic moment of having elected an American president of color in 2008, the first such man inaugurated in the United States of America. This means that we also welcome the honor of having the first African American first lady ever in our nation's history.

Michelle Obama became the first African American first lady of the United States when her husband Barack Obama was sworn in as the 44th president of the United States. The 2008 presidential election yielded some monumental results and changes for the entire American electorate. A nation that had for over three centuries held people of African descent in bondage finally elected someone of African descent to be president of the United States of America. In a nation where African American women have had to struggle against both racial and gender discrimination, it is humbling to have a woman of African American descent in this unprecedented public role, living in the White House and working side-by-side with the president.

Michelle Obama has defied the negative stereotype of the angry Black woman. Educated, articulate, and a purveyor of a strong family unit, she is an inspiration to many. In July 2008, Michelle Obama and then senator Barack Obama were depicted on the cover of *The New Yorker* magazine. The cover displayed Mrs. Obama carrying an assault rifle. The controversial cover was debated in many circles as being demeaning and negatively stereotypical of Black women. Having successfully juggled the roles of wife, mother, and attorney, Mrs. Obama is a role model for all women. She epitomizes what is best about our great nation—commitment to family, community, and country. She proves that by putting your best foot forward, a woman in America—even a woman of color—can indeed have it all.

African American women have struggled for generations to define themselves in the unique paradox of being both Black and female. Although African American women are disproportionately affected by issues such as discrimination, poverty, and health concerns, the sharing of mutual issues of concern is beneficial to women of all ethnicities. In the 2008 presidential election, progress toward racial harmony in this nation was made. There was also some progress toward the empowerment of women.

African American women have been on a complicated and bumpy journey politically. Their aims have not yet been adequately met as a result of numerous political and social movements in American history. Despite tirelessly asking for a seat at the head table of American politics, and not receiving one, they continuously demonstrate their loyalty and determination to the aim of having a viable voice for Black women and their interests in the electoral atmosphere. African American women make up the majority of the African American electorate. In the 2008 presidential election, 95 percent of Black voters voted for Barack Obama and as in previous years, more Black women turned out to vote than Black men.[4] In 2008, 64.4 percent of Black women turned out to vote in the presidential election, compared to 56.4 percent of Black men.[5] In the 2004 presidential election, 59.8 percent of Black women came out to vote compared to only 51.8 percent of Black men.[6] In the year 2000, 57.3 percent of Black women voted for president compared to only 50 percent of Black men and in 1996, 53.9 percent of Black women voted compared to 46.6 percent of Black men.[7] The same trend continued in 1992, where 56.7 percent of Black women actually voted compared to 50.8 percent of Black men.[8] Among Asians, Hispanics, and Whites, female voters outnumbered male voters in recent elections. The difference in voter turnout rates between genders was greatest among Blacks.[9] This was evident even in the 1970s when Shirley Chisholm, the first African American woman to be elected to the U.S. Congress, correctly surmised that many households in the Black community are headed by women and Black women register to vote in greater numbers than Black men.[10] Time and again, they have demonstrated their influence as a powerful voting bloc in key national elections. African American women vote rather consistently, and they usually vote in large percentages. They have historically been a key constituency for the Democratic Party. "African American women are the base of the Democratic Party," Daniella Gibbs says.[11] Gibbs is a former deputy communications director for the Democratic National Committee. For example, in 2004 during the presidential election, 94 percent of Black women voted for Democratic presidential candidate, Al Gore, compared to only 6 percent that voted for Republican candidate George W. Bush.[12] Studies conducted of the 1992, 1996, and 2000 presidential elections demonstrate that Black women are the most loyal Democrats of any demographic group.[13] In 1992, 86 percent of Black women voted for Bill Clinton compared to 44 percent of White women.[14] In 1996, 89 percent of Black women voted for Bill Clinton compared to 42 percent of White women.[15] What would be the political after effects if Black women decided to support other political parties in larger numbers? What would happen if they voted as diversely as they are as a populace? Would they have a more effective way of having their core issues addressed?

The women's rights movement excluded many Black women, as did the civil rights movement, from its leadership. Men dominated the major public leadership roles within the civil rights movement, relegating many women to roles that were not in the forefront of the movement. Many observers noted that the majority of the focus of the civil rights movement was on the oppression of Black men. Meanwhile, White women dominated the women's suffrage movement. The women's suffrage movement, as well as the civil rights movement, gave African American women an unprecedented opportunity to become an active and engaged part of the American political landscape. These movements, however, failed to adequately address the specific needs of Black women. Black feminism emerged partially out of Black women's dissatisfaction with both the civil rights movement and mainstream feminism. Some might argue that bonds between members of the same race may be stronger than bonds between members of the same gender, but is there more solidarity between Black men and Black women than between Black women and White women?

Where Is the African American Woman's Voice?

As of 2011, there are no African American women in the U.S. Senate. Only one African American woman, Carol Moseley Braun, has ever been elected to the Senate. However, currently there are 15 African American women members of the 112th Congress in the U.S. House of Representatives, all members of the Democratic Party. These distinguished women are: Barbara Lee, Karen Bass, Laura Richardson, and Maxine Waters of California; Corinne Brown and Frederica Wilson of Florida; Donna Edwards of Maryland; Yvette Clark of New York; Marcia Fudge of Ohio; Eddie Bernice Johnson and Sheila Jackson Lee of Texas; Eleanor Holmes Norton of the District of Columbia; Donna Christensen of the Virgin Islands; Teri Sewell of Alabama; and Gwen Moore of Wisconsin. Christensen and Holmes Norton are two of the nonvoting delegates in the House. No African American woman has ever served as governor of any state in the country. Examine the statistics on women and African American women who hold statewide elective office, and the evidence is clear that these sorts of numbers hold true at the state level as well. This trend is also evident in the examination of several state statistics of women and African American women who hold elective office. For example, Pennsylvania's voting age population is over 50 percent female and approximately 10 percent African American. Neither group has comparable representation among top state and federal offices. There is one woman and one African American in the 21-member congressional delegation in the state of Pennsylvania, and there has never been an African American or female governor in the state.[16] Only approximately 15 percent of the 253 seats in the Pennsylvania legislature are filled by women.[17] Pennsylvania ranks 43rd in the country in female representation in their state legislature.[18]

To analyze this phenomenon properly, it would be necessary to look back at the extensive history that African American women have had in the women's suffrage movement as well as their role in the movement for civil rights. During this time period, the U.S. Congress was controlled by Southern Democrats who generally opposed civil rights progression for Blacks. Southern sympathizers felt that giving the vote to women would add to the numbers of Black voters. Numerous women's suffrage groups decided that in order to maintain the critical support of southern White females, African American females needed to be sacrificed. The Nineteenth Amendment was passed, which gave White women the right to vote but did not give African American women that same right.

As far back as 1890, prominent civil rights activist and women's suffrage advocate Mary Church Terrell spoke of the dual handicap of both race and gender for the African American woman. Terrell worked very hard to get Black women actively involved in the women's rights movement and to bond with White women in a universal sisterhood.[19] Terrell used several strategies to convince African Americans to join the cause and White suffragists to support their entry.[20] These strategies included definite ways to bring Black and White women together for the same aim. She was one of the thousands of African American women who fought for the rights of all women during the women's suffrage movement. However, progress during that time was considerably slow.

African American women faced the obstacle of gender bias in the civil rights movement. Not to be deterred, Black women were pivotal soldiers in the movement for social justice and equal rights, dealing simultaneously with the obstacles of both race and gender within the struggle. Thousands of Black women quietly pushed for racial justice in the background of the civil rights movement. Despite their efforts, many African American women felt discrimination from racial bias in the women's suffrage movement and also felt oppression from gender bias within the civil rights movement.

The women's rights movement is linked with the struggle for racial equality in the United States. Both movements have challenged the established institutional barriers to social, political, and economic empowerment for women as well as African Americans in this country. A huge gain for the women's movement, which resulted from the civil rights movement, was the Civil Rights Act. The Civil Rights Act of 1964 provided for the protection of rights for both African Americans and women, making the passage of the historical legislation a victory for both African Americans as well as women. It prohibited discrimination on the basis of race, gender, religion, or national origin.

In 2008, for the first time in our nation's history, an African American man and a White woman vied for the nomination of a major political party for the office of the presidency of the United States. Then an African American man and a woman ran on opposing presidential tickets for the first time in history from major parties. Concurrently, Cynthia McKinney, an African American female, won the Green Party nomination for president. Many African American women currently report that a candidate's race or gender may not have played enough of a role to surpass the relevance of a candidate's position on contemporary issues that are critically important to this dual identity group.[21] Would they vote for a candidate who looked like them or for someone who felt their pain and shared their experiences and identifies and represents the issues that they were most concerned about?

The fact is that the history of racial discrimination in this country has been so much more pervasive than gender discrimination for many African American women. Since slavery, African American women have had to prioritize the fight against racial discrimination above the fight against gender discrimination for their survival. The brutality of racially motivated murders and lynchings made this prioritizing an absolute necessity. The evidence is clear, that Black women have at times been discriminated against even within their own communities. Unfortunately, too many African American women have, at one time or another, viewed being both Black and female as a double negative when it comes to workplace and political ambitions.

In the historic 2008 presidential election, African American women had a unique and unprecedented choice in perhaps selecting gender over race or race over gender. African American women have consistently demonstrated themselves to be the most dependable demographic within the Democratic Party. These women can be viewed as the grand prize, so to speak, in some crucial state contests. African American women are credited with helping Senator Barack Obama win the South Carolina Democratic primary, establishing him for the first time as the Democratic frontrunner during the race for the Democratic presidential nomination. These women are credited with making a difference, because in South Carolina they make up the majority of Black voters. Black women were positioned to make the difference in primaries where the makeup of the members of the Democratic Party is heavily African American. According to the Joint Center for Economic and Political Studies, African American women make up 60 percent of the registered Black electorate. This demographic of women have played a huge role in the party nomination process in the 2008 presidential election year by accounting for at least 57 percent of the vote in every primary and caucus within the Democratic Party.

Many observers express the notion that Black women voters do not get the respect that they deserve for emphasizing their impact within the African American electorate.[22]

An analysis of the voting trends of African American women in the two presidential elections prior to 2008 indicated that African American women had the potential to have a huge impact on the 2008 presidential election. African American women were key players in handing Al Gore victories in the electoral -vote–heavy states of California and New York during the 2000 presidential election. In that election, 94 percent of African American women voted for Democratic presidential candidate Al Gore, making them "the single strongest group in the country," says David A. Bositis, senior research associate at the Joint Center for Political and Economic Studies; 85 percent of African American men voted for Al Gore. Through this support from the African American electorate and African American women in particular, Gore was able to win in states such as New York and Michigan. Six out of 10 African American voters in that election were women.[23]

In 2004, African American women made up 7 percent of the total electorate and two-thirds of the African American electorate; 69 percent of Blacks were registered to vote.[24] In that presidential election, 88 percent of African Americans supported the Democratic presidential nominee, Massachusetts senator John Kerry, with 75 percent of non-Black women supporting him as well.[25] Kerry garnered 51 percent of the overall women's vote.[26]

Some numbers suggest that 35 million eligible women did not vote in the previous presidential election. African American voters made up 22 percent of the total votes for Senator Kerry.[27] This was an increase from the 18 percent of African American voters who voted for Al Gore.[28] African American female voters were a larger share of the electorate and voted for Kerry in larger numbers, so their contribution to Kerry's numbers was 9 percent higher.[29]

In the 2006 midterm elections, 91 percent of African American women voted for Democratic candidates, the same year that the Democrats were able to take back control of Congress.[30] This voting bloc represented 6 percent of the total electorate in the elections. In a sample of African American women who were surveyed following the midterm elections, 90 percent of the women who were surveyed replied that they looked most favorably upon New York senator Hillary Clinton for president (90%), followed by Illinois senator Barack Obama (61%) and former senator Johns Edwards (53%) as potential presidential contenders.

African American women were poised to come full circle electorally in this presidential election. The trends from recent presidential elections indicated that this dual identity group would have a huge impact on the election outcomes in key states. According to the Pew Research Center, African American women made a huge and substantial impact on the presidential election of 2008. That election had the highest number of African American female voters than any other presidential election in history. States that have a large African American electorate would impact heavily in the election outcomes according to preliminary poll results. These women had a fervent feeling that they had so much to gain politically from producing a strong voter turnout on election day. Their hopes and aspirations were for their collective advancement economically, socially, and politically as a result of electing one of their own—albeit a member of their racial group or a member of their gender group.

African American women, just as they have in the past, still face a tremendous uphill and continuous battle to fight off the perils of poverty, disproportionate health ills, and racial and gender discrimination. Households headed by women in the United States have the highest poverty rates. African American households have higher rates of poverty than White households in the United States. The impact of both racial and gender discrimination is evident in the statistics that indicate that Black women earn significantly less money than men and than women of several other ethnicities. Despite the fact that, according to the Department of Education,

African American women earn 67 percent of all bachelor degrees earned by Blacks, 71 percent of all of the masters degrees, and 65 percent of all of the doctorate degrees earned, African American women even earn less money than African American men.[31]

African American women have specific constituent interests at heart when they enter the voting booth. For instance, in 2006, the rate of new human immunodeficiency virus (HIV) infection for Black women was nearly 15 times as high as that of White women and nearly 4 times that of Hispanic/Latina women.[32] African American women are disproportionately affected by acquired immunodeficiency syndrome (AIDS). AIDS infection is a looming health crisis within the African American community. Add this to the fact that according to the Centers for Disease Control only about one in five Black women has health insurance, and it becomes clear that access to adequate health benefits is paramount for many Black women, large numbers of whom are unmarried mothers. These women are often in the arduous position of raising children as single parents, and obtaining health benefits for children is of utmost importance to them. They need a president who can relate to the importance of these critical issues in their everyday lives. Many feel that an African American president is better able to understand the abyss of racial discrimination and will be compelled to address the issue. Others feel, however, that a female president will be better able to relate to motherhood and health issues that are akin to those who have had the same experiences.

No matter who they think might be the best candidate for giving them what they need, these mothers want to be able to provide adequately for their children. They want to live in safe neighborhoods with access to adequate local schools and community programs and activities for their offspring. They want adequate job opportunities that offer equal pay to provide their children with security and stability. They desire to give their children the opportunity for a solid education and adequate health care. Many feel that a woman candidate may be more sympathetic and, thus, best in addressing these particular concerns and acting on them once in office, particularly since many female candidates are mothers themselves.

The intersectionality of race and gender in American politics is a relatively new phenomenon. At no other point in our history have African American women been able to choose between candidates from major political parties from both their racial and gender identities in a single presidential election. The question during the 2008 presidential election was asked continuously: Were African American women going to support an

African American candidate or a female candidate? Time and again, the responses were inconclusive. Where did African American women stand on the issues most important to them? What historical precedent, if any, determined which identity (race or gender) more African American women ultimately ended up identifying with? This unique and now influential voting bloc and dual identity group can no longer be ignored as it has been in decades past. Many African American women are looking beyond the layers of race and gender in regards to the selection of candidates to support for elective office. What did that mean in such a critical election year? How would the American political landscape be impacted? Would African American women predictably embrace the nomination of either a woman or an African American as one of their own?

Chapter 2

A Look Back

And frankly, being a woman I think gives me a slightly different take on a lot of issues and on a lot of the solutions to the problems we face.

—Senator Carol Moseley Braun

The Center for American Women in Politics (CAWP) reports that over 12,000 people have served in the U.S. Congress, but only less than 2 percent of these people have been women. The CAWP also reports that the number of women in elective office on the federal level has not changed dramatically in more than 25 years.

Women's suffrage leader Elizabeth Cady Stanton was the first woman to run for a seat in the U.S. House of Representatives. At the time when Stanton ran in 1866, she was not even eligible to vote. She garnered only 12 votes out of the 12,000 that were cast. Citizens during this time period were annoyed by a woman running for an elective office, but they were just as appalled by the mere suggestion that women should be granted the right to vote at all.

The first woman to serve in the U.S. Senate was Georgian Rebecca Latimer Felton in 1922. She served for only 24 hours since she was appointed to fill a vacancy. Hattie Wyatt Caraway was the first woman elected to the Senate in 1932, following a stint as an appointee to the Senate to fill a vacancy caused by the death of her husband Senator Thaddeus Caraway. Hattie Caraway served in the Senate until 1945 but failed to get reelected to her seat. Thirty-five women have since served in the U.S. Senate, with only one being African American, former Senator Carol Moseley Braun.

The first woman to be elected to the U.S. House of Representatives was Jeanette Rankin of the state of Montana in 1916. She was the first female member ever in the U.S. Congress. Rankin's election to the 77th Congress preceded the ratification of the Nineteenth Amendment, so support from women voters did not have a big impact on her unprecedented election. She did work vigorously to gain the right to vote for women in her home state of Montana, where women were granted that right in 1914. An early advocate for child care for women workers, Rankin rallied for women's suffrage upon her entry into office.

In 2006, Congresswoman Nancy Pelosi became the Speaker of the House of Representatives in the 110th Congress, making her the first woman and the first Italian American to hold the Speakership. She was the House Minority Leader from 2002 to 2007 and the House Minority Whip, the first woman to hold those positions as well. Prior to that, she represented the 8th Congressional District of California in the House of Representatives. She is the highest-ranking woman to ever hold office on the federal level of government. As Speaker of the House, she was third in line to the succession to the presidency.

Also unprecedented on the federal level was Geraldine Ferraro's nomination by a major political party as a candidate for vice president of the United States in 1984. Ferraro was a member of the U.S. House of Representatives from New York City's 9th District. She was chosen as the first female candidate ever for vice president of the United States. Ferraro ran on the Democratic Party ticket with former vice president Walter Mondale who was the presidential candidate that year. As a member of the House of Representatives, Ferraro had fought hard for the passage of the Equal Rights Amendment and she sponsored the Women's Economic Equity Act, which would end pension discrimination against women. Ferraro was not elected vice president, but she did forge a trail of historic precedence. Twenty-four years later, Alaska governor Sarah Palin became the first woman to run as the vice presidential nominee for the Republican Party when she ran on the presidential ticket with Senator John McCain in 2008. Palin became the second woman to run on a presidential ticket from a major political party and the first Alaskan to do so.

Miriam A. Ferguson became the first woman governor in the United States when she became the governor of Texas in 1925. Nellie Tayloe Ross followed by becoming governor of Wyoming. They were both wives of former governors. Ella Grasso was the first governor who was not the wife of a former governor when she became governor of Connecticut in 1974. Arizona and Connecticut are the only two states to have women elected as governors from both major political parties. Twenty-eight states have still never had a female governor and no African American woman has ever served as a governor of any state in the United States.

Soon after the women of Kansas gained the right to vote in city elections, Susanna Salter became the first woman elected mayor of an American town in Argonia, Kansas, in 1877. Legend has it that a group of men nominated her as a joke and she ended up getting two-thirds of the vote. In 1971, Patience Sewell Latting, the first woman on the Oklahoma City Council, was elected mayor of Oklahoma City, becoming mayor of the largest city in the country ever headed by a woman at that time. Latting's background included activism with the local Parent Teacher Association and the League of Women Voters. She was the first woman to be elected mayor of a city with a population of over 350,000 people.

African American women, like African Americans in general, supported the Republican Party originally, since it was the party of President Abraham Lincoln. Following slavery, Blacks became supporters of the Republican Party to fight against the White supremacists mired within the Democratic Party during the Reconstruction era. The Republican Party took leadership in the ratification of the Thirteenth, Fourteenth, and Fifteenth Amendments to the Constitution. This changed with the presidency of Franklin Delano Roosevelt, who was the first president to have African Americans as advisors, who were referred to as his Black cabinet. These individuals were highly trained academics and professionals who were at the top of their individual fields. Through his New Deal programs, there were set asides to help African Americans in housing, employment, and education, who as a group were hit particularly hard by the economic disparities of the Great Depression. African American support for the Democratic Party was solidified with civil rights legislation and the passage of the Voting Rights Act in 1965. This shift in party affiliation was a factor in the later election of numerous female and minority candidates throughout the nation, including the election of Shirley Chisholm, the first Black woman to be elected to the House of Representatives.

Following the passage of the 1965 Voting Rights Act, African Americans began voting in large numbers throughout the country.[1] The Voting Rights Act outlawed the disenfranchisement of African American voters through discriminatory voting practices long used for the suppression of minority voter participation, particularly in the South. The Act's purpose was to eliminate hardball tactics such as the implementation of the grandfather clause and literacy tests to prevent African Americans from exercising their constitutional right to vote. It was during this time that more African Americans began to enter elective office as a result of the influx of newly registered African American voters throughout the nation. Between

1970 and 2001, the number of Black public officials increased from 1,469 to 9,101.[2]

African American Women Trailblazers in American Politics

Carol Moseley Braun was the first African American woman to serve in the U.S. Senate. She was elected in 1992 from the state of Illinois. Moseley Braun became the first African American female U.S. senator when she was sworn in on January 3, 1992, during the Year of the Woman in Congress when there were record numbers of women, particularly women of color, elected to both the House of Representatives and the Senate following the Clarence Thomas and Anita Hill scandal. Some suggest that the 1992 Year of the Woman phenomenon was spurred by the astringent questioning of law professor Hill by an all-male, all-White Senate Judiciary Committee. Moseley Braun became the first female senator to defeat an incumbent when she defeated Alan Dixon in the Democratic primary. The thought of an African American female senator was so foreign that when attempting to secure a Capitol Hill photo ID, the card she received read spouse instead of senator. Moseley Braun was instrumental in striking down a congressional patent design to the insignia of the United Daughters of the Confederacy, which she fought by reminding members on the Senate floor that it would be disrespectful to the legacy of African Americans to support the insignia. She helped to guide the legislative branch in focusing on issues relating to women and minorities. No other African American woman has been elected to the U.S. Senate since Moseley Braun's historic election.

Shirley Chisholm of New York was the first African American woman elected to the U.S. House of Representatives in 1968 from the 12th Congressional District in New York. Previous to that, she was elected to the New York state legislature in 1964. In 1972, Chisholm became the first woman as well as African American woman to mount of serious candidacy for the presidency of the United States of America within a major political party. When mounting her candidacy, Chisholm declared, "I stand before you today as a candidate for the Democratic nomination for the presidency of the United States. I am not the candidate of black America, although I am black and proud. I am not the candidate of the women's movement of this country, although I am equally proud of that. I am not the candidate of any political bosses or special interests. I am the candidate of the people."[3]

Her declaration stands as a testimony to the combined interests of African American women, some of whom may have wanted her to represent their specific interests. Chisholm garnered 151 delegate votes at the 1972 Democratic National Convention that was held in Miami, Florida. Incidentally, she received a broad base of support, including strong support from feminists and women's advocacy groups despite being underfinanced and underorganized. Supporters of Chisholm included feminist pioneer Gloria Steinem, who ran to be elected as one of Chisholm's delegates. Chisholm was a strong advocate of issues that are traditionally important to women, including education, health care, and childcare. During her first term in office, she sponsored a bill to finance day care facilities. Chisholm was one of the founders of the Democratic Select Committee, which eventually came to be known as the Congressional Black Caucus, in January 1969. The group functioned as a lobbying arm to the Congressional Democratic Party. The caucus focused on issues that disproportionately affected African Americans and the urban minority poor. The Caucus's issues included education, welfare reform, and minority business development. Chisholm's legacy is that she inspired a new generation of leaders, both female and African American, including current California representative Barbara Lee, who is a former campaign worker for Chisholm. Her efforts paved the way for future African American female candidates for president including Lenora Fulani, who was the first African American woman to appear on the ballot in all 50 states.

The first African American woman to serve as mayor of a major American city was Sharon Pratt Dixon in Washington, DC. She served as the mayor of the nation's capital from 1991 to 1995. Shirley Franklin served as mayor of Atlanta from 2002 to 2010, becoming the first Black female mayor of a major southern city. Other Black female mayors of major American cities currently include Stephanie Rawlings-Blake of Baltimore, Maryland and Marilyn Strickland of Tacoma, Washington.

Stagnant Progression for Female Elective Officeholders

Analyses that examine the reasons for the slow progression of women in elective office indicate that the candidacies of women are affected by numerous cumbersome factors. Incumbency is a significant factor, since statistics indicate that approximately 80 percent of incumbents are reelected to office. Since men are the majority of elective office holders, incumbency is a huge advantage to them. Some evidence suggests that term limits would lead to larger numbers of women legislators.[4] By increasing elective office turnover, the argument lingers that open-seat opportunities would have a better chance of being created for more women.

Campaign fundraising is also another obstacle for many female candidates since females running for elective office have much more difficulty raising money to run for office than male candidates. Oftentimes it is the primary reason why female and minority candidates do not successfully get into elective office. Former U.S. senator Carol Moseley Braun had difficulty raising money for her 2004 presidential run and she ended up dropping out of the presidential race before the Iowa caucuses. Senator Hillary Clinton raised $212 million for her historic 2008 presidential run, the most money raised by any female candidate for elective office in U.S. history.[5]

More often than not, voters do not seem to consider female candidates as qualified as male candidates. Many voters openly express their skepticism of females being able to handle the sometimes rigorous demands of elective office. This factor alone makes female candidates much less competitive, particularly when they are running directly against male candidates. This was the case for Governor Sarah Palin in 2008. Being the mother of five children, the youngest being under a year old and having Down's syndrome, Palin was often chastised for pursuing such an important office instead of being home raising her children. Detractors and supporters alike questioned whether or not Palin should be spending time away from her children to run for vice president. The attacks became even more scathing when it was announced that Palin's 17-year-old daughter was pregnant. The fact was that two of the candidates on the major party tickets, Barack Obama and Sarah Palin, were working parents of young children, but Palin as the only mother, took the majority of the criticism from the double standard for not choosing to remain home with her children. Many potential voters doubted whether Palin could balance home and running the country, given some of the family issues that were confronting her at the time, which included dealing with the pregnancy of her teenaged daughter.

Senator Hillary Clinton's 2008 presidential campaign was a contradiction to this—particularly following the departure of the other candidates for the Democratic presidential nomination when it was a race between her and Obama. Clinton was able to demonstrate that a woman could be competitive when competing in a one-on-one race against a man. Many voters felt that she was strong enough to be the commander-in-chief and for some it had the opposite effect. It turned off many voters who viewed Clinton as too strong and polarizing.

The pipeline theory surmises that since fewer women pursue elective office, it results in fewer women being elected to office so therefore more women must put themselves forward to run for elective office. Further studies indicate that women are less likely than men to consider running for office and they are less likely to begin the process of launching a campaign to run for office due to the obstacles imposed upon women candidates. In a sample of potential candidates for office, the majority of the respondents noted that levels of recruitment for female candidates, perceptions of electability, and traditional family dynamics affects their desirability and decision to pursue elective office.[6] Women who have more household responsibilities and who have families are less likely to pursue elective office. Women who generate lower household incomes are also less likely to run for public office. These dynamics make the ambition to attain elective office more problematic for women than for men.

Chapter 3

Racial Bias within the Women's Suffrage Movement

We hold these truths to be self-evident: that all men and women are created equal.

—Elizabeth Cady Stanton

African Americans or women were not matters for consideration during the Second Continental Congress in the year 1776. First Lady Abigail Adams wrote a letter to her husband addressing the condition of women: "Remember the ladies and be more generous and favorable to them than your ancestors. Do not put such unlimited power into the hands of husbands. Remember, all men would be tyrants if they could."[1] President Adams's reply was: "As to your extraordinary Code of Laws, I cannot help but laugh."[2]

The goal of the abolitionist movement of the 18th and 19th centuries was to make the practice of slavery illegal in the United States of America. The movement attracted many followers from various religious and cultural backgrounds, including Quakers and Unitarians. From its onset, this movement combined race, class, and gender differences. The gender differences worked to result in the exclusion of women from the World Anti-Slavery Convention in 1840. The female attendees were secluded behind a curtain at the convention. Several prominent women abolitionists went on to form their own societies as a result of their exclusion.

During this time period in America, women could not vote or hold elective office. Women could not sign contracts nor sue in a court of law. They could not even serve on juries. Virtually all of a woman's property would become her husband's possession. Married women could not gain custody of their children in the event of divorce. Rarely could women divorce their husbands even if they were abused. Women during this time period had limited educational opportunities and few occupations were open to women, the main ones being teaching and nursing.

Abolitionists Elizabeth Cady Stanton and Lucretia Mott developed the idea to start a women's rights movement following the exclusion of the female abolitionist delegates to the World Anti-Slavery Convention. Stanton's husband was a prominent abolitionist in the antislavery movement and Mott founded the Philadelphia Female Anti-Slavery Society in 1833. Women were very involved in the creation of antislavery societies. These women combined their interest and commitment to both abolitionism and women's suffrage. They used the skills they acquired from working in the abolitionist movement to organize a movement for social change for women in America.

The first Women's Rights Convention was held in New York in July 1848. Approximately 300 women and men attended this convention in Seneca Falls, the location of a significant number of reformers during this time period. The first day of the convention was set aside exclusively for women. At the time, a woman speaking publicly was frowned upon. So prominent African American abolitionist Frederick Douglass was asked to speak at the convention following the first day since women speaking publicly was looked upon with disdain during this time period. The declaration that came from the convention was written by Elizabeth Cady Stanton and it declared that "all men and women are created equal."[3] The right to vote became the major focus of the women's rights movement.

Many saw parallels between the women's rights movement and the abolitionist movement. Elizabeth Cady Stanton, Harriet Tubman, Lucretia Mott, and Sojourner Truth all embraced both abolitionism and feminism, fighting simultaneously for the rights of Blacks and women. There was however growing tension between Black female abolitionists and White suffragists on how to promote both the freedom of Blacks and the oppression of women synchronously. Abolitionists would not allow women to sign resolutions or vote in meetings. This hypocrisy frustrated women and propelled them to solidify their own movement.

Following the end of the Civil War, female abolitionists wanted suffrage for both Blacks and women. The Thirteenth Amendment abolished slavery and the Fourteenth and Fifteenth Amendments were ratified, which granted citizenship and protections to Blacks, resulting in half their battle being won. All of these amendments were a collective legislative action that impacted a paradigm shift in the civil rights in this nation. The Thirteenth Amendment, which prohibited slavery in the United States, was adopted as an amendment to the Constitution in December of 1865. Section 1 of the Thirteenth Amendment states: "Neither slavery nor involuntary servitude, except as a punishment for crime whereof the party shall have been duly convicted, shall exist within the United States, or any place subject to their jurisdiction."

The Fourteenth Amendment, which laid the groundwork to establish citizenship for former slaves, provides a broad description for the criteria for citizenship. The first section of the amendment states: "All persons born or naturalized in the United States, and subject to the jurisdiction thereof, are citizens of the United States and of the State wherein they reside. No State shall make or enforce any law which shall abridge the privileges or immunities of citizens of the United States; nor shall any State deprive any person of life, liberty, or property, without due process of law; nor deny to any person within its jurisdiction the equal protection of the laws." In July 1868, the Fourteenth Amendment became a part of the U.S. Constitution.

The Fifteenth Amendment established that a citizen cannot be prevented from voting due to race or previous condition of voluntary or involuntary servitude. The amendment was ratified in February 1870. Section 1 of the amendment says, "The right of citizens of the United States to vote shall not be denied or abridged by the United States or by any State on account of race, color, or previous condition of servitude." The amendment makes no mention of gender.

Moreover, these amendments did not address the plight of women. Susan B. Anthony and Elizabeth Cady Stanton both opposed the Fifteenth Amendment because it did not also grant women the right to vote. Some Black women, such as writer Frances Ellen Watkins Harper, sided with Black men for not wanting to risk the passage of the Fifteenth Amendment by demanding that voting rights for women be added to it. Harper was, however, an advocate for Black women who said that she wanted African American women to be a "sharer in the social and moral development of the race."[4] On the other side, women such as Sojourner Truth advocated just as vociferously for the right for Black women to vote as for Black men. Black men of the day seemed to have had less opposition to women's voting rights than White men. Many men of the day viewed the granting of voting rights to women as insulting to the institution of marriage and to the man's traditional role as head of the household. Some Black men though supported and worked for the enfranchisement of women. Abolitionists such as Frederick Douglass supported suffrage for women, but felt that getting the right to vote for Black men was more pressing at that particular time. When reminded that Black women shared the same harsh indignities as Black men, Douglass's response was "Not because she is a woman, but because she is Black."[5]

Stanton and Anthony led efforts to defeat both the Fourteenth and Fifteenth Amendments primarily because the of the Fourteenth Amendment's focus on male voters. For the first time, the proposed amendment would insert the word male into the U.S. Constitution. This outraged some women's suffragists. Opposition from these women's suffragists angered Black women, who felt that opposition to the amendment was a betrayal to the fight for racial equality. The trend continued during Reconstruction when Black feminists supported the passing of the Fifteenth Amendment, again spurning the protests of White female suffragists. The continual struggle between suffragists and civil rights leaders caused huge divisions between White and Black suffragists.

Emancipation did not bring equality in employment. In most U.S. cities, Blacks were limited to lower-paying jobs, primarily due to racial discrimination. Within this paradigm is the revelation of how, at the time, the differing experiences of women during this time period set up the distinctions between women of the different socioeconomic classes based on concentration of wealth and exploitation of labor.[6]

In the post-slavery era, Black women mainly worked as domestics and teachers in colored schools. Many African American women, educated and uneducated, were a willing part of the women's suffrage movement during the antebellum period. The National Association of Colored Women (NACW) was formed by Black women in 1896. Prominent members included the leading Black female activists of the day—Harriet Tubman, Ida B. Wells-Barnett, Frances E. W. Harper, and Mary Church Terrell as its president. Terrell, the daughter of former slaves, would serve as president of the Bethel Literary and Historical Society, one of the most prominent colored organizations in the country during that time period. She became the first Black woman to serve on any city board when she was appointed to the District of Columbia Board of Education. Mary Church Terrell spoke of the dual handicap of both race and gender for Black women: "A white woman has only one handicap to overcome, a great one, true, her sex; a colored woman faces two-her sex and her race." The NACW promoted both women's suffrage and civil rights agendas.

The NACW became the primary vehicle for race leadership for Black women.[7] They established both state and local chapters. Members taught classes for women in various disciplines and coordinated volunteer efforts in group homes and hospitals. The organization viewed race, gender, and class as interlocking paradigms with independent variables that could not be solved independently. In their minds, "a race could rise no higher than its women."[8] Their premise was that if they improved the condition of Black women, then they improved the condition of their race.

The NACW included a component that pushed for the advancement of women's suffrage laws. The Alpha Suffrage Club of Chicago was founded in 1913 by Ida B. Wells-Barnett to work exclusively on issues of women's suffrage. Wells, an antilynching crusader, suffragist, and journalist, took members of her club to the nation's capital to march in a suffrage parade. The organizers of the march, the Congressional Union, led by Alice Paul, asked the Black women to march in a segregated unit in the back of the parade. Mary Church Terrell had also brought together a group of African American women to be part of the parade. Terrell and others decided just not to march in the parade. As the parade began, Barnett decided not to comply and she jumped from the crowd and joined the White delegation.[9] This was just one example of how African American women at times faced discrimination from those working within the women's suffrage movement.

Stanton and Anthony created the National Woman Suffrage Association (NWSA) in 1869. The NWSA was created in part due to the split within the women's suffrage movement over the Fifteenth Amendment not addressing the plight of women's rights. Black women worked actively with the National American Woman Suffrage Association (NAWSA). NAWSA's aim was more focused toward the passage of laws supporting women's suffrage on both the local and state levels. The NWSA at times discouraged Black women's clubs from affiliating themselves with the NAWSA. Abolitionist Frederick Douglass became an honorary member of the NAWSA. Susan B. Anthony requested that Douglass not attend NAWSA's annual meeting in 1894, to be held in Atlanta, Georgia, so that southern White women would not be obstructed from joining the organization. Anthony inquired to Ida B. Wells-Barnett as to whether or not her actions were in error. Wells replied, "Uncompromising yes," for "I felt that although she may have made gains for suffrage, she had also confirmed White women in their attitude of segregation."[10] The NWSA would eventually merge with another women's organization into NAWSA. Southern members of the NAWSA pushed just for the enfranchisement of White women only. Feminist icon, Elizabeth Cady Stanton, publicly expressed her opposition to the Fifteenth Amendment applying to Black men, but not to women: "Shall American statesmen . . .

so amend their constitutions as to make their wives and mothers the political inferiors of unlettered and unwashed ditch-diggers, bootblacks, butchers and barbers, fresh from the slave plantations of the South?"[11]

As noted in chapter 1, since the U.S. Congress was controlled by Southern Democrats who generally opposed civil rights progression for Blacks, Southern sympathizers felt that giving the vote to women would consequently add to the numbers of Black voters. Certain women's suffrage groups decided to sacrifice African American women in order to maintain the critical support of Southern White females. Mary Ann Shad Cary was prompted to form the Colored Women's Progressive Franchise Association as an auxiliary to some White suffragists opposed to integration. Adella Hunt Logan, who could pass as White, would attend the meetings of the NAWSA to keep Black women up to date on the organization's operations.

Growing numbers of Black women supported the women's suffrage movement despite the racial discrimination that they faced within the movement. There were prominent Black suffragists such as Frederick Douglass, Ida B. Wells-Barnett, Mary Church Terrell, and Adella Hunt Logan. Logan, a professor at the Tuskegee Institute, was also a writer who advocated that Black women were victims of racism as well as sexism. She held lengthy discussions concerning women's suffrage at the Tuskegee Woman's Club. She also wrote about women's rights in the National Association for the Advancement of Colored People's *Crisis* magazine.

Elizabeth Cady Stanton and Susan B. Anthony led efforts to defeat both the Fourteenth and Fifteenth Amendments, because of the Fourteenth Amendment's focus on male voters. For the first time ever, the proposed amendment would add the word male into the U.S. Constitution. This outraged some women's suffragists. Opposition from these women's suffragists angered Black women, who felt that opposition to the amendment was a betrayal to the fight for racial equality. The trend had its beginnings during Reconstruction when Black feminists supported the passing of the Fifteenth Amendment, spurning the protests of White female suffragists.

The coalition of women's suffragists began to unravel. There was a divide between factions that supported either voting rights for women first or voting rights for Blacks first. Some saw the women's issue as a deep Anglo-American cultural issue. There were fractures in the movement along racial lines, class lines, and interests. Lucy Stone and Julia Howe, who in fact supported the ratification of the Fourteenth and Fifteenth Amendments, began the American Woman Suffrage Association. Eventually both the

NWSA and the AWSA merged into the National American Woman Suffrage Association (NAWSA) in 1890.

The Nineteenth Amendment would grant all women of the United States the right to vote. Jim Crow laws and Black voter disenfranchisement prevented most Black women from the full protections of the Nineteenth Amendment. Lynchings, poll taxes, and other forms of intimidation impugned many Blacks from voting or even registering to vote. Typical disenfranchisement measures that were used to deter Black voters included tax qualifications, grandfather clauses, educational tests, etc. Black women partnered with the National Association for the Advancement of Colored People (NCAA) to fight these tactics. The leading women's suffrage groups were not always willing to support the efforts of Black women voters in the South. As a result, Black women began to pull away from the women's suffrage movement and instead moved toward racial injustice issues that would focus on the mobility of African Americans.

Black suffragists became disillusioned with the women's rights movement because they felt that they never received full inclusion into the suffrage movement. In fact, organizations such as the National American Woman Suffrage Association excluded Black women from their organization. They found that existing racism did little to improve the status of their lives despite the gains made by the women's rights movement. New York state elected its first Black state legislator shortly after the passage of the amendment.

Colorado became the first state to grant women the right to vote in 1893. The ratification of the Nineteenth Amendment, along with economics, created the momentum for the women's rights movement. Due to changes in the American economy during this time period, more women had to seek work outside of the home. As women experienced inequalities in terms of job opportunities and compensation, women began to think about and mobilize themselves politically.

Women during this time did not move easily into elective offices primarily because the political parties of the day would not promote them. More women consequently joined the suffrage movement. Many observers note that the enfranchisement of women voters did not immediately impact the number of elected female officials nor did it bring a remarkable change to the political landscape.

There were many social, cultural, and political differences that prevented Black women from reaping the full benefits of the women's suffrage movement. The lack of a concerted effort to bridge the divide between White women and Black women during the struggle for women's suffrage left a deep scar in the solidarity of abolitionists and suffragists. African American women felt that they were a separate minority within White feminist organizations. Historically, Black female abolitionists placed racial issues as a priority, thereby in part leading to a separation between Black and White female abolitionists. Many argue that the perception of what affects only women is diminished when compared to concerns that include the consideration of its effect on men. Black women are not referenced directly in the U.S. Constitution. The violence and intimidation perpetuated through Jim Crow laws made it almost impossible for Black women to enjoy the privileges and protections of the Nineteenth Amendment for decades. It would take the civil rights movement to enfranchise completely the rights of many African American women, particularly in the South.

Chapter 4

Gender Bias within the Civil Rights Movement

Women hold up half the world—in the case of the civil rights movement, it's probably three-quarters of the world.

—Julian Bond

As with the women's suffrage movement, African American women would play a significant role in another political movement for equal rights in America. The civil rights movement focused on ending racial segregation in American life, suppressing voter disenfranchisement and ending racially motivated violence. It was a movement that was defined by the struggle to end what was viewed as second class citizenship for African Americans in the United States. The civil rights movement spanned several decades, beginning primarily in the 1950s. The beginnings of the civil rights movement included Rosa Parks's iconic refusal to move to the back of a Montgomery Alabama city bus, hence igniting the Montgomery bus boycott, the first significant event of the American civil rights movement.

One of the culminating events during the civil rights movement was the 1963 March on Washington. This march was the result of a coalition of civil rights organizations of the time including the Southern Christian Leadership Conference (SCLC), the Student Nonviolent Coordinating Committee (SNCC), the National Association for the Advancement of Colored People (NCAA), the Brotherhood of Sleeping Car Porters (BSCP), and the National Urban League (NUL). The focus of the march was the passage of civil rights legislation, the desegregation of public schools, and the eradication of racial discrimination. The platform of the 1963 March on Washington included 10 demands. Some of the demands included the following:[1]

1. Passage of meaningful civil-rights legislation at this session of Congress—no filibustering;
2. Immediate elimination of all racial segregation in public schools throughout the nation;
3. A big program of public works to provide jobs for all the nation's unemployed, including job training and a placement program;
4. A federal law prohibiting racial discrimination in hiring workmen—either public or private;
5. $2-per-hour minimum wage, across the board, nationwide;
6. Withholding of federal funds from programs in which discrimination exists; and
7. Enforcement of the Fourteenth Amendment, reducing congressional representation of states where citizens are disenfranchised.

During the historic March on Washington, no woman gave a major address. Legendary entertainer Josephine Baker only gave brief remarks when she introduced the Negro Women Fighters for Freedom, which included civil rights icon Rosa Parks. Thousands of women attended the march, but women who had major leadership roles in the civil rights movement were not invited to meet with President John F. Kennedy following the historic march. Many women in the movement felt that the omission of women from this important meeting was intentional and symbolic of their struggle for visibility within the movement.[2]

Rosa Parks is unquestionably the most notable of the women of the civil rights movement. It seems that so many other courageous and remarkable women have been unceremoniously written out of the history books of this time period. Ella Baker, Vivian Malone Jones, Septima Poinsette Clark, and Fannie Lou Hamer are just a few of the women who put their lives on the line alongside the men of the movement and made major contributions to further the movement. The wives of the leaders of the movement, primarily Coretta Scott King, Myrlie Evers Williams, and Betty Shabazz, became the most visible women of the civil rights movement. Women such as Fannie Lou Hamer were continuously beaten and jailed for trying to register to vote, marching in protest rallies, and participating in bus and business boycotts. Ella Baker was a longtime leader in the Southern Christian Leadership Conference. Vivian Malone Jones courageously enrolled in the segregated University of Alabama in 1963.

These women were not deterred from working in the movement despite the male-dominated atmosphere. The common thought was that African American men, often emasculated by larger society, adapted patriarchal roles within the civil rights movement. These women became the unsung heroines of the modern-day American civil rights movement.

The Women's Political Caucus and the Beginning of the Civil Rights Movement

The Women's Political Council (WPC) was formed in 1946 as a civic organization for professional African American women in Montgomery, Alabama. The WPC was the first group to officially call for a bus boycott in Montgomery. Women who were instrumental members of this council included Jo Ann Robinson and Mary Furr Burks. Burks, chairperson of Alabama State College's English Department, was the group's first president. Robinson succeeded Burks as president as the group's focus turned from education to fighting the bus abuses occurring throughout Montgomery. The women of the Montgomery bus boycott decided on a three-tier approach, which included voter registration and interviewing candidates for office, protesting public transportation and city park segregation, and educating students about democracy and the importance of adult literacy.[3] Robinson wrote a letter to Mayor Gayle of Montgomery in May of 1954 and informed him that several local organizations were becoming interested in conducting a bus boycott in the city. The WPC decided that when the proper person was arrested, then the boycott would commence. Claudette Colvin was a 15-year-old who was arrested for refusing to give up her seat on a Montgomery bus to a White person, which at the time was a violation of local law. The WPC and other local organizations began discussing the start of the proposed boycott. Shortly thereafter, it was determined that Colvin was pregnant and since there was concern that conservative Blacks in Montgomery would not support the boycott because of this, these plans were abandoned. Several others were arrested after Colvin, but the boycott was not begun until the arrest of Rosa Parks in December of that year. On the evening that Parks was arrested, Jo Ann Robinson circulated a flyer throughout the community that read:

> Another woman has been arrested and thrown in jail because she refused to get up out of her seat on the bus for a white person to sit down. It is the second time since the Claudette Colvin case that a Negro woman has been arrested for the same thing. This has to be stopped. Negroes have rights too,

for if Negroes did not ride the buses, they could not operate. Three-fourths of the riders are Negro, yet we are arrested, or have to stand over empty seats. If we do not do something to stop these arrests, they will continue. The next time it may be you, or your daughter, or mother. This woman's case will come up on Monday. We are, therefore, asking every Negro to stay off the buses Monday in protest of the arrest and trial. Don't ride the buses to work, to town, to school, or anywhere on Monday. You can afford to stay out of school for one day if you have no other way to go except by bus. You can also afford to stay out of town for one day. If you work, take a cab, or walk. But please, children and grown-ups, don't ride the bus at all on Monday. Please stay off all buses Monday.[4]

The Montgomery Bus Boycott

The Montgomery bus boycott opposed Montgomery's local laws that upheld segregation on its public transportation systems. Black citizens refused to ride city buses. Across the nation, Black churches and organizations raised money to support the Montgomery boycotters and collected shoes for the citizens of Montgomery who had to walk great distances to get to work and school as a result of the boycott. Many had to walk everywhere they went. This boycott gave the civil rights movement one of its first victories and catapulted the Reverend Doctor Martin Luther King Jr. into the national spotlight.

With the success of the start of the historic Montgomery bus boycott, the Montgomery Improvement Association was created. Martin Luther King Jr. was elected its president and Jo Ann Robinson served as a member of its executive board. The historical boycott lasted approximately one year until the Supreme Court eventually ruled the Montgomery's policies of racial segregation of its public transit system unconstitutional.

Ella Baker and SNCC

African American women also played a major role in the creation of the Student Nonviolent Coordinating Committee. SNCC was created as an organization where student activists could share information and experiences. Ella Baker was critical in the creation of the organization by coordinating the April 1960 conference at Shaw University in Raleigh, North Carolina, that resulted from the creation of SNCC. It was Baker's ideas of student engagement that gave the movement the momentum it needed for continued effectiveness of the sit-in movement.

Many brave men and women worked within the organization, but the SNCC had to rely largely on the work of women. Women who became active in the lunch counter sit-in movement of 1960 became leaders in the transformation of SNCC from a coordinating office into a cadre of militant activists dedicated to expanding the civil rights movement throughout the South.[5] The Black Women's Liberation Committee was created from the efforts of SNCC in the late 1960s. Many SNCC volunteers put themselves at great risk when participating in the Freedom Rides in the Deep South. The states in the Deep South included Georgia, Mississippi, Alabama, South Carolina, and Louisiana.

Ella Baker was the director of the Southern Christian Leadership Conference until she became disillusioned by the organization's inability to appoint women in the organization's leadership. Baker attributed her departure from the SCLC to problems with its male leadership seeming to be disinterested in her ideas. Ella Baker virtually ran the Southern Christian Leadership Conference but she had to relinquish decision-making authority to the male leadership.[6] SNCC's influential organizing groups included a significant number of Black women. "The movement of the fifties and sixties was carried largely by women since it came out of the church groups," Baker explained. "It is true that the number of women who carried the movement is much larger than that of men."[7]

Fannie Lou Hamer and the Fight for Racial Equality

Fannie Lou Hamer was perhaps the best known of the female civil rights leaders drawn into the movement through SNCC. After attending a SNCC meeting in 1962, Hamer attempted to register to vote. Following her try at voter registration, Hamer was given a choice by her proprietor to remove her name from the voter lists or leave the plantation where she had worked for the past 18 years. As part of her punishment by local authorities, she was subsequently arrested and was the victim of a horrific beating in jail following her arrest. She was then prompted to get more involved in SNCC and eventually became the SNCC field secretary. Hamer was a key player in organizing the Mississippi Freedom Summer for SNCC in June 1964. Mississippi Freedom Summer was a drive designed to get as many Black voters as possible registered in the state of Mississippi. At the time, there were virtually no registered Black voters in the state. Volunteers would be severely beaten and sometimes murdered as was the case with the infamous Chaney, Goodman, and Schwerner murders during the Mississippi Freedom Summer of 1964. The participants in the Freedom Summer campaign were mostly White and residents of northern states, and Hamer proclaimed her belief that the civil rights movement should be multiracial in its nature.

The Mississippi Freedom Democratic Party was created to challenge the all-White Mississippi delegation to the Democratic National Convention as the delegation was not inclusive to minorities. This drew national attention to the plight of Black voters in the state of Mississippi. If the Mississippi Freedom Democratic Party were to succeed, there were feelings that the Southern delegations would desert the party in favor of Republican candidate Barry Goldwater. Hamer was invited to make her case before the Credentials Committee of the Democratic National Convention. President Lyndon Johnson called a press conference to distract the networks away from Hamer's testimony, and when speaking to his advisors, reportedly referred to her as "that illiterate woman."[8] The networks aired her testimony anyway, and the Credentials Committee received thousands of letters and phone calls supporting the Mississippi Freedom Democratic Party. Operatives would offer a compromise to Hamer and the Mississippi Freedom Democratic Party that would give them two seats. Hamer and her supporters rejected this and future negotiations were made without Hamer's involvement. Although they failed to receive the number of seats that they felt they deserved, the Mississippi Freedom Democratic Party helped to influence the Democratic Party to adopt a clause that would require equality in the makeup of state delegations to the Democratic National Convention in 1968. Hamer would be seated at the 1968 convention where she became an outspoken critic of the Vietnam War. Hamer continued working for the Mississippi Freedom Democratic Party and other civil rights causes, such as Martin Luther King's Poor People's Campaign. Hamer would go on to become one of the most proactive and outspoken voting rights activists in our nation's history.

Septima Clark and the Gender Bias within the Movement

Septima Clark was a pioneer in civil education for African Americans. Clark was one of 11 Black teachers who was fired for being a member of the National Association for the Advancement of Colored People (NAACP). Clark began adult literacy programs within what was termed citizenship schools with the help of civil rights activist Bernice Robinson. The purpose of the schools was to help Blacks get full citizenship through education. Clark maintained that women's participation in the citizenship efforts were part of the quest for civil and women's rights.[9] Literacy tests became a deterrent that segregationists and opponents of the civil rights movement used to prevent Blacks from registering to vote. Blacks would be required to read long passages of the Constitution and to interpret their meaning. Since many Blacks in the South were illiterate, this prevented most Blacks from exercising their right to register to vote. The schools that Clark worked to set up taught thousands of Blacks to read and write and were attended by and taught in by such individuals as Rosa Parks and Fannie Lou Hamer. These schools also taught Blacks about the structure of government and democracy as well as community organizing, and tactics in resistance and struggle. She set up schools in stores, beauty salons, and the homes of private citizens. Former Atlanta mayor Andrew Young, who served as Clark's supervisor at SCLC, said that the Citizenship Schools were the foundation of the civil rights movement, "as much responsible for transforming the South as anything anybody did."[10] In 1957 at the request of Martin Luther King, she went to work for the Southern Christian Leadership Conference where she worked on the planning of demonstrations and marches. In 1965, Dr. King insisted that Clark accompany him to Sweden to receive the Nobel Peace Prize. He wanted to see that Clark would receive just as much credit for her work in the civil rights movement as he did. King remarked that Clark had a tremendous influence on his nonviolent philosophy and it was he who coined her as the "mother of the movement." Clark was convinced that the violence advocated by some was not the direction that the movement should have gone toward.

Clark wrote that the men on SCLC's executive staff didn't listen to her. She wrote that they liked to send her to organize with other civil rights organizations, because she was really good at getting people to listen to what she has to say. "But those men didn't have any faith in women, none whatsoever. They just thought that women were sex symbols and had no contribution to make."[11] Following her years in the civil rights movement, Clark became an active feminist following her conclusion that she and other female workers within the movement had experienced sexism.[12] Clark described one example: "If you watch the movie 'From Montgomery to Memphis,' you'll notice that they don't mention one woman going through there. Not one. You almost never see their role put down in any of the reports about the Movement. You just get 'Dr. So-and-so from Alabama State College did such-and-such.'" She called sexism "one of the weaknesses of the civil rights movement."[13] She described her various experiences with gender bias within the movement: "I found all over the South that whatever the man said had to be right. They had the whole say. The woman couldn't say a thing."[14] Clark, like Ella Baker, held formal leadership positions within women's organizations. By 1970, in large part due to the contributions of courageous and committed women such as Septima Clark, over one million African American voters had been registered in the South.[15]

Women Demonstrating within the Movement

Women who played an active part of the sit-in movement were critical to the progression of the fight for civil rights. They helped to sustain the freedom rides through the imprisonment of other student freedom riders. Civil rights workers were barraged constantly with threats of violence and intimidation. These workers and their families often became victims of drive by shootings, fire bombings, and arson. Black women were notorious for holding bake sales and supplying food for rallies and protest gatherings. Women generally attended demonstrations in larger numbers than men. It is well documented that the civil rights movement grew out of the Black church. The Black church was the most prominent institution in the Deep South, capable of reaching large segments of the Black populace.[16] Women for the most part, attend church in higher numbers than men, so naturally more women would have been a part of a movement that was an extension of the church. Black women continued to quietly push for racial justice in the background of the movement.

Black women were pivotal soldiers in the movement for social justice and equal rights, dealing with the obstacles of both race and gender in the struggle. According to women who did achieve prominence through the civil rights movement, sexism and authoritarian views of leadership prevented women from assuming leadership of any of the movement organizations.[17] Amy Jacques Garvey argued that Black women should be in the forefront of the struggle for Black Americans as well as for Black women having a primary role in the fight for Black liberation through the organization, the Universal Negro Improvement Association, which her husband founded.[18]

Another African American female trailblazer who also worked within the civil rights movement was the Reverend Dr. Anna Pauline Murray was a civil rights activist who went on to become a cofounder of the National Organization for Women (NOW) in 1966, the nation's most prominent feminist organization, which was created in the model of the National Association for the Advancement of Colored People. Murray would go on to become one of the country's most prominent feminists.

The effort to keep Black women from the forefront of the civil rights movement is seen by some to have been a reflection of the standards of that particular time period. "In some ways it reflects the realities of the 1950s: There were relatively few women in public leadership roles," said Julian Bond, a civil rights historian at the University of Virginia and chair of the NAACP. "So that small subset that becomes prominent in civil rights would tend to be men. But that doesn't excuse the way some women have just been written out of history."[19]

Women such as Ella Baker, a longtime organizer with the Southern Christian Leadership Conference; Vivian Jones, a civil rights activist who enrolled at the University of Alabama in defiance of Governor George Wallace; and Daisy Bates, the teacher who guided the Little Rock Nine to integrate Little Rock High School in 1957 were not given full credit by the assessment of most civil rights historians. Dorothy Height has been quoted as saying, "Black women are the backbone of every institution but sometimes they are not recognized as even being there, even in the Civil Rights movement."[20]

African American women remained active in the ongoing phases of the feminist struggles in the United States. Malcolm X summed up his personal observations and view on the contributions of women to the movement for racial equality in this country: "And I frankly am proud of the contribution that our women have made in the struggle for freedom and I'm one person who's for giving them all of the leeway possible because they've made a greater contribution than many of us men."[21] Women unarguably played a significant role in instigating women's activism in the struggle for civil rights. Despite their roles, their contributions to the struggle were oftentimes overlooked in large part because they were women.

The women's suffrage movement and the civil rights movement are inextricably linked by their commonality. Both the women's rights movement and the civil rights movement fought for justice for women and African Americans. The contributions and values of many African American women shaped the strategies and the ideology of the civil rights movement. As with the abolitionist movement, many White women became inspired by the fight for justice from African Americans and began a new women's rights movement that focused on the Equal Rights Amendment, reproductive rights, domestic violence, and employment. By the 1980s, the racial profile of feminism began to change as women activists in the African American, Asian American, Latina, and Native American movements began to speak out about the racially exclusionary aspects of feminism as well as their own perspectives on women's rights.

Chapter 5

The Shortcomings of Black Feminism

*Did St. Paul but know of our wrongs and deprivations, I presume he would make
no objections to our pleading in public for our rights. Again; holy women minis-
tered unto Christ and the apostles; and women of refinement in all ages, more or
less, have had a voice in moral, religious and political subjects.*

—Maria Stewart (1833)

Many African American women felt the wounds from the discrimination
of racial bias in the women's suffrage movement and also felt the oppression from gender bias within the civil rights movement. The failures of
these movements to specifically address the needs of Black women led to
the development and creation of a new kind of feminism. It was during this period that Black women began to ponder the impact of gender
oppression and the stagnant progress of Black women. The feelings of discontent from Black women as a result of racial and gender oppression from
both movements formulated the political and social theories of Black feminism. Black feminism emerged in the 1970s in the United States.

Black feminism is feminine consciousness through an African American perspective. Black feminism espouses the premise that race, gender,
and class interchangeably are related. The contemporary Black women's
movement developed in the 1970s. A number of factors contributed to
Black women's feelings that they need a feminism of their own. First of
all, from its inception, the U.S. civil rights movement had espoused strict
gender roles for Black women. Second, Black nationalist organizations
that formed after the initial phase of the civil rights movement, such as
the Black Panthers, were also sexually oppressive, Third, Black women

suffered in society as a whole from racial, gender, sexual, and economic oppression. This new Black feminist movement spoke to the problems of racism, sexism, *and* classism. It focused on such issues as sexual harassment, aging, lesbian and gay discrimination, and reproductive rights. Black women wanted to confront the oppression, and sometimes the brutality, of gender and racial discrimination. This dual identity group of women must struggle for equality both as females and as African Americans, and they have needs and challenges that are distinct from White women and Black men.[1]

Few Black women in the 1970s desired to be identified as feminists. Many Black women began to rebel against the established thought that racial discrimination was the primary obstacle for Black women. Some began to define Black feminism as a process of struggle that empowers women and men to actualize a humanistic vision of community. Maria Stewart, considered by some to be the mother of Black feminism, challenged Black women to reject the negative images of Black womanhood.[2] Stewart, both an abolitionist and feminist, maintained that racial and sexual oppression were the fundamental causes of the impoverishment of Black women.[3] She argued for the need for education for Northern Blacks, particularly girls. Emancipation from oppression has been an ongoing theme from Black feminist thought. The mobilization of African American women would be based in part on the ideas espoused by Maria Stewart. She chastised Blacks for not being proactive in the uplifting of their own condition. Stewart's ideas sought to urge African American women to free themselves from the oppression of both racism and sexism. She encouraged women to have a voice in political affairs. Stewart would eventually become disillusioned by the discrimination that she faced from members of her own and community and promptly ended her public career.

Nevertheless, Stewart contributed greatly to the legacy of Black feminism. Following the civil rights movement, Black feminist organizations began to spring up across the country. This organization, which was short-lived, was created in 1973 in New York. The National Black Feminist Organization (NBFO) focused on many issues including reproductive rights, health care, day care, violence against women, lesbian and gay rights, aging, and sexual harassment. Some Black feminists could not agree upon which racial ideology would hasten the empowerment of Black women. Some wanted to be integrationalists while others followed a more nationalistic point of view. White women should be seen as the natural allies of Black women. Differences among Black women, along with the infusion of

Black lesbian ideology, splintered the Black feminist movement. One woman espoused her position as this:

> All women suffer oppression, even white women, particularly poor white women, and especially Indian, Mexican, Puerto Rican, Oriental and Black American women whose oppression is tripled by any of the above-mentioned. But we do have female's oppression in common. This means that we can begin to talk to other women with this common factor and start building links with them and thereby build and transform the revolutionary force we are now beginning to amass.[4]

Outside controversies and conflict within the organization eventually led to the resignation of the president and most of the members of the board of the NBFO. The NBFO fell out of existence as did many of the other leading Black feminist organizations. Numerous organizations similar to the NBFO did not outlive the 1970s and 1980s. Despite these obstacles, the legacy of Black feminism lives on.

In 1974, the Combahee River Collective (CRC) in Boston was founded with a Black lesbian perspective. The name came from the Combahee River where Harriet Tubman as a woman, planned a military campaign to free hundreds of slaves. A group of Black feminists came together to assess the state of Black feminism and they created a statement based upon their assessment. The CRC statement emphasized that they held the fundamental and shared belief that "black women are inherently valuable, that . . . [their] liberation is a necessity not as an adjunct to somebody else's but because of [their own] need as human persons for autonomy" and expressed a particular commitment to "working on those struggles in which race, sex, and class are simultaneous factors in oppression."[5] The statement describes "contemporary black feminism [as] the outgrowth of countless generations of personal sacrifice, militancy, and work by our mothers and sisters" such as Sojourner Truth, Harriet Tubman, Frances E. W. Harper, Ida B. Wells-Barnett, and March Church Terrell, as well as thousands upon thousands of unknown women, and situates itself as "actively committed to struggling against racial, sexual, heterosexual, and class oppression, and see as our particular task the development of integrated analysis and practice based upon the fact that the major systems of oppression are interlocking. The synthesis of these oppressions creates the conditions of our lives."[6]

Membership in organizations such as these included Black women from various socioeconomic backgrounds to focus on issues pertinent to all of them collectively. Challenging the oppression within the African American culture is at times viewed as divisive and counterproductive to efforts to solidify the works of African American men and women collectively.

As a result of the efforts of Black feminists, many colleges and universities currently offer courses that specifically address the contributions and efforts of African American women. These courses examine the history of Black women from slavery through Reconstruction, Jim Crow, the civil rights movement, and on to the development of a contemporary Black feminism. Readings and discussions in such courses usually include the examination of activist strategies for accomplishing social change, grassroots principles of community organization, and the structure and division of male female roles in Black communities. Feminist theory also adapted its rationale to begin to include an examination of how classism and racism affect the lives of women of all ethnicities, the theory being that Black women were also affected by socioeconomic constraints as well as being affected by discrimination because of their race.

Women play a critical role in many facets of American society. For decades, being wives and mothers were considered women's most significant roles in society. Eventually, though, women began to categorically accomplish a reevaluation of the traditional views of their roles in American society. Once women were allowed personal and intellectual freedoms, they were able to make significant achievements and contributions to American society. Instead of beginning with gender and adding other variables such as class, religion, race, sexual orientation, and age, Black feminist ideology recognizes those distinctive systems of oppression as being part of one overarching structure of domination.[7] Hindering African American women from voting, excluding African Americans and women from public office, and withholding equitable treatment in the criminal justice system all substantiate the public subordination of women.[8]

The condition of involuntary servitude impacts all subsequent roles and relationships that African American women have inside and outside of these various communities. Those opposing Black feminism argue that racism is the primary mode of oppression facing women of color and that there is a greater need to focus on that perceived larger human rights struggle. Detractors have also accused the feminist movement of threatening the unity of the African American male and female. Detractors have also accused the feminist movement of threatening the unity of the African American male and female. It is a common belief that Black men and women should fight racism through a united front and to separate the aims of Black men and women would be a deathblow to the struggle of the African American fight for racial equality. The quagmire for Black women sometimes came down to choosing between standing with African American men in the shared struggle against racial oppression or standing up for their own interests as females both inside and outside of the African American community.

Black feminism became the feminist ideology that gave light to the unique history of the racial and gender oppression of Black women. The Black feminist theory espouses that most African American women experience racism, but that social status differences among African American women impact how and to what extent that racism is experienced. Out of the growing frustration with the civil rights movement and the feminist movement, more Black women manifested their disenchantment with these movements by attempting to carve a different path through which they could propel issues and concerns unique to the double jeopardy of their race and gender. The variables that have compounded African American women's journey with the challenges of dual identity oppression have separated African American women from natural alliances.

Although African American women made more gains following the passage of the Voting Rights Act in 1965, the interchangeable web of economics, societal conjecture, and politics function as a highly effective system of social control that is designed to keep African American women in a subordinate place.[9] The Black feminist movement, however, proved inadequate in addressing issues that adversely affected the overall quality of life for African American women. Black women must reexamine the importance of coalitions with African American men, White women, and other groups with distinctive standpoints.[10] Maria Stewart called for the unifying of Black women to foster activism and more autonomy over their self-determination. She felt the Black women had to increase their level of political activism and that would in effect increase their political autonomy, making Black women a larger shareholder in decisions that would great enhance their quality of life.

Black feminist theory advocates that empowerment of Black women would represent empowerment of all people since it would require an end to racial, gender, and class oppression. Black feminism became a movement for African American women's independence and self-reliance. The goal of this movement was to embrace a consciousness that was both race-conscious and feminist. Women share common experiences that are different in context from those that affect racial groups. Black feminism is rooted in the need that developed for Black women to begin to assert their inherent right to speak as both African Americans and as women.

Chapter 6

The 2008 Presidential Election: Substance or Symbolism?

Could a woman really serve as Commander-in-Chief? Well, I think we answered that one. And could an African American really be our President? Senator Obama has answered that one.

—Hillary Clinton

African Americans had traditionally voted for Republicans since the days of President Abraham Lincoln when most Blacks identified themselves as supporters of the Republican Party. Many Blacks shifted their political alliance to the Democratic Party during the presidency of Franklin Roosevelt after finding Roosevelt's policies and programs advantageous to their community. This shift was solidified during the Kennedy administration due in large part to the administration's commitment to civil rights, despite the fact that numerous Democratic Congressman did not vote for the passage of the 1964 Civil Rights Act. As far as the issue of civil rights was concerned, the issue didn't go down party lines, but regional lines. It was where legislators were from that usually determined their positions on civil rights issues. The Democratic Party had a major base in the South, and many Southern voters were pro-segregation and anti-civil rights. However, there were many Northern liberals in the Democratic Party, most notably Hubert Humphrey of Minnesota, who were pro–civil rights, so a number of Southern Democrats begin to split from the Democratic Party, such as Strom Thurmond and George Wallace, began to run as third party Dixiecrats. So the significant Democratic base in the South was slipping. Since Nixon inaugurated the Southern Strategy to switch White Southerners unhappy with civil rights legislation to the Republican Party, the party has consistently acted against the aspirations of Black Americans. Part of Nixon's law and order platform was to take a more moderate position on civil rights. While this helped him win in the South and throughout the country, it turned off many minority voters, not just Blacks, and that is why most Black voters tend to vote for Democrats. The Democratic Party espouses more policies and programs geared toward the impoverished and the working class, and since a disproportionate amount of African Americans live below the poverty line, they tend to vote significantly more for Democratic Party candidates for elective office.

Forty-one percent of Black voters responded to a 2008 survey saying that a female candidate for president should get their vote. Among African Americans, 30 percent of the respondents report that Oprah Winfrey's endorsement would influence their candidate of choice on election day. Twenty-eight percent of the respondents reported that they that they would be more likely to vote for a woman.[1]

The ultimate attainment of political power in the free world is becoming president of the United States. In 2008, the nation was caught up in the frenzy of seeing if the next president of the United States would for the first time ever be a woman. Many political observers and pundits wondered endlessly about the possibility of having an African American become president. What would this symbolize to our great nation? What would be the substance of such historic precedent? Would it mean that America has overcome its ugly history of both racial and gender oppression? What would electing either a woman or an African American man to the presidency mean for the millions of African American women living in the United States of America?

After eight years of the Bush administration, Americans seemed eager to embrace a change in the executive branch of the government. President Bush's approval ratings were some of the lowest for any president in history and many respondents to polls taken at the time responded that they felt that the country was not headed in the right direction. Many voters questioned the legitimacy and effectiveness of the Iraq War and there was much uncertainty in regards to the nation's economy. In the last month of his presidency, just 13 percent of American adults responded that they strongly approved of the way that George W. Bush performed his job as president.[2] It was an ideal time for candidates from diverse backgrounds to run for the highest office in the land. The people were demanding drastic change.

Despite the fact that women make up half of the electorate in America, many women feel that not only are they underrepresented in elective office, but also that their issues are underrepresented by their elected officials. Many women see and feel the inequality that still exists to this very day, despite great strides made since the feminist movement of the 1970s began. It appears that that many male voters would be too intimidated to vote for a strong female for president. Some women themselves have suggested that a woman may be incapable of holding a position of power. In a survey of Democratic voters taken in 2008, the majority of the Democratic women polled thought that the election of a woman to the presidency would be more significant than that of the election of an African American to the presidency, which was what the majority of Democratic men polled thought.[3] Women made up almost 6 in 10 voters in Democratic primaries and caucuses during the 2008 presidential campaign.[4] Still, Obama ended up winning the Democratic Party nomination.

The question of identity politics and its role in this election were a new phenomenon. Would a Black President be more inclined to address issues of concern to African Americans? Historically, there has been difficulty getting much focus on the issues of African American women. As far back as 1955, Mary McLeod Bethune had created the National Council of Negro Women out of her concern that Black women were putting their energy into building male-dominated organizations and were not focusing enough on issues vital to women of color. These issues remain today.

The 2008 election raised the question about whether Black America should vote for candidates who proclaim that there is no Black America or White America, but there is just one America. It seems that no African American candidate could get to become the presidential nominee of a major political party by addressing serious issues of concern to primarily Black constituents, the prevailing thought being that addressing said issues would alienate White voters who do make up the majority of the overall electorate. These issues include skyrocketing African American unemployment and school retention rates. The disparities of workplace salaries between African Americans and other ethnicities is another issue that has ignited controversy in the political atmosphere.

In the beginning of his presidential campaign, Black voters experienced some ambivalence towards Senator Barack Obama due to their perceived notion that he was not electable and concerns for his safety if he were elected.[5] Barack Obama was a product of community organizing efforts in Chicago, Illinois. He graduated from Harvard Law School, where he was the first African American president of the prestigious *Harvard Law Review.* He was elected to the U.S. Senate in 2004 where he represented the state of Illinois. Son of a White mother and a Kenyan father, Obama became a shining symbol for the new postracial politician. Promoting an agenda of change, Obama quickly resonated with voters who desired such change and a renewed sense of hope for a new direction for the country.

The 2008 Presidential Election

Women outvoted men in every state primary during the 2008 presidential election year. According to the Joint Center for Economic and Political Studies, African American women currently make up 60 percent of the registered Black electorate.[6] African American women have consistently demonstrated themselves to be the most dependable demographic within the Democratic Party.

This demographic was instrumental in handing Al Gore key victories in the electoral vote–rich states of California and New York in the presidential election of 2000. African American women were viewed as the grand prize, so to speak, in some of the critical state primaries in 2008. African American women are credited with helping Senator Barack Obama win the South Carolina Democratic primary. They would make the difference in primaries where the make-up of the members of the Democratic Party in those states is heavily African American. These states included North Carolina, South Carolina and Virginia.

It is commonly believed that many African American women have placed race above gender when it came to the choice between voting for the first African American president in Senator Obama and the first female president in Senator Clinton. Barack Obama made big gains in the overall number of women voters primarily because African American women began voting for him in very large numbers.[7] This was the case in the South Carolina primary where Obama received a huge advantage from that state's primary win in the overall race for the Democratic nomination for president. Twenty-eight percent of the voting age population in the state of South Carolina during the 2008 Democratic primary was African American.[8]

Several CBS News polls taken in January 2008 prior to the South Carolina Democratic primary indicated that Hillary Clinton held a substantial 15-point lead over Barack Obama among African American women early on in the presidential race.[9] This was noted to be largely due to the emotional connection that African Americans felt toward former president Bill Clinton. Many held the assumption that the connection would continue with the former first lady, Hillary Clinton. Many anticipated that having a member of the Clinton political dynasty in the White House would mean that Bill Clinton's influence would play a significant role in any new Clinton administration. The expectation was that Hillary *could* win. However, once Barack Obama became the first African American to win the Iowa caucuses, more African Americans gave his candidacy a second look. The view, real or perceived, was that America would now accept an African American commander-in-chief. Many African Americans began to believe that Obama had a serious chance of winning the nomination, largely due to his win during the Iowa caucuses. That perception resonated with millions of African American voters and they slowly began to support Obama's quest for the nomination. Obama also benefitted from a surge in support as a result of an endorsement by Oprah Winfrey, whose support was key in his successful primary victories in several states, including the state of South Carolina.

Key Issues for African American Women

The status of addressing contemporary issues confronting the African American community was very important to African Americans during this election cycle. These issues directly affect the quality of life for millions of African Americans. Despite unprecedented access to higher education and employment, African Americans remain more economically, socially, and politically disadvantaged than other ethnic groups.

Overall, about 55 percent of African American women consider themselves to have a moderate view of most issues of the day, with 23 percent seeing themselves as liberal and 22 percent seeing themselves as conservative.[10] African American women's primary issues of concern generally include health care access, employment, discrimination, and education. Secondary issues include but may not be limited to political representation, crime, socioeconomic status, and race relations. Comparatively, African American women earn less salary than men and women of other ethnicities. HIV and AIDS have had a devastating effect on the African American community. According to the National Institutes of Health, AIDS is now the number one killer of African American women aged 25 to 44. African American women are currently the fastest-growing segment of the population to contract the AIDS virus and develop the disease. This is a situation that is distinct to African American women as a demographic and pushes these issues to the forefront for many African American female voters.

According to ABC News, 70 percent of African American women in America are single. These women are more than likely to be heads of their households and addressing the aforementioned issues is crucial for their continued survival and progress. Studies also reveal that single women who head households are more likely to live below the poverty line. Seventy percent of single mothers live in poverty, many having a household income of less than $13,000 annually.[11] As with many voting demographics, positions on issues relevant to these particular voters carry a lot of weight in their determination as to which candidates they will support and vote into office.

Growing Voting Blocs within the Electorate

The largest-growing voting bloc in the country is unmarried women, and this group outnumbers African Americans and Hispanics put together. African American women make up about 18 percent of this group.[12] In total, 72 percent of African American women are unmarried.[13] Women tend to register to vote in higher numbers than men. When unmarried women vote, they tend to vote Democratic. Seventy-five percent of unmarried African American voters are African American women.

This group of unmarried women tends to be less educated and to earn lower incomes. Fifteen percent of all single African American women have earned a college degree.[14] According to the *New York Times,* in 2007, 70 percent of professional African American women were unmarried. Other statistics show that Black women are five times as likely to be single than White women. Over half of these women have incomes under $30,000 annually compared to only 13 percent of these women who make more than $75,000 annually.[15] The candidates they tend to vote for closely represent issues that directly impact their daily lives. This seems to drive their choice of candidates for which they will ultimately vote for elective office. Their core issues usually center on economic concerns, health issues, and education, since a significant number of these women are single mothers. This same report cites 58 percent of these same women having to pay more for their health care costs.[16] Their views on education, affirmative action, employment and housing are reflective in the candidates that women of color seem to support for elected office. According to Women's Voices Women Vote, unmarried African American women are more likely than any other group of unmarried women to vote. They cite economic prosperity as the major concern for this particular group of voters.

In the 2000 presidential election, 94 percent of African American women voted for Democratic presidential candidate, Al Gore, making them "the single strongest group in the country," says David A. Bositis, senior research associate at the Joint Center for Political and Economic Studies;[17] 85 percent of African American men voted for Al Gore.[18] Through this support from African Americans and African American women in particular, Gore was able to win in states such as New York and Pennsylvania.

In 2004, African American women made up 7 percent of the total electorate and two-thirds of the African American electorate, and 69 percent of Blacks were registered to vote.[19] In the presidential election that same year, 88 percent of African Americans supported the Democratic presidential nominee, Senator John Kerry, with 75 percent of non-Black women supporting him as well.[20] Kerry garnered 51 percent of the overall women's vote.[21] Some statistics of eligible voters suggest that 35 million eligible women did not vote in the 2004 presidential election. African American voters made up 22 percent of the total votes for Senator John Kerry. This was an increase from the 18 percent of total votes for Al Gore in 2000.[22] African American women voters were a larger share of the electorate and voted for Kerry in larger numbers so their contribution to Kerry's numbers was 9 percent higher.[23]

In the 2006 midterm elections, 91 percent of African American women voted for Democratic candidates.[24] This voting bloc represented 6 percent of the total electorate in the election. In a sample of African American women who were surveyed following the midterm elections, 90 percent of the women who were surveyed replied that they looked most favorably upon Senator Hillary Clinton for president followed by Senator Barack Obama (61%) and former senator Johns Edwards (53%).[25]

Is It Substance or Symbolism?

Some political naysayers and potential Obama supporters didn't feel that Obama brought enough experience to the table to be the next president of the United States, citing that he had only served in the Senate for two years before launching his bid for the presidency. There were political pundits who suggested that Senator Clinton brought too much negative baggage from President Clinton's White House years. Regardless of what reservations one may have held against either candidate, Democratic voters were eager to see what the election of either would do for their constituencies. The logical assumption, flawed or not, was that women voters could identify more with a female candidate, since it was assumed that women candidates would be more likely to support issues important to women such as daycare, jobs with equal pay, and reproductive rights.

With a collective interest in similar issues, should Black women as a demographic have been merged with the overall women's vote? Many believe that women of all racial groups legitimately share many of the same issues and concerns, such as education, health care, reproductive choice, domestic abuse, child care, and compensation equity. Research supported this premise as well. Women of all backgrounds, ethnicities, etc. tend to share concern collectively over many of the very same issues. The difference comes apparently when issues of race are of concern. Key issues for African American women do include those of other women, such as health care and education, but they are also concerned about minimum wage increases, and HIV/AIDS. According to the Centers for Disease Control, one in five African American women doesn't have health insurance benefits. This statistic has a huge impact on women of this ethnic and gender group, economically and politically. They are attracted to candidates who are committed to ensuring that they have adequate and equal access to health care. This is an extremely hot button issue in today's political climate and was a major issue for candidates in the 2008 presidential election. Voters will look towards candidates who will address their issues around the cost of health care or the lack of health care benefits.

The reality is that African American women, as a dual-identity group, are inseparable from both natural identities of race and gender. All Americans, including African American women, could take tremendous pride in the election of either an African American or a woman to the highest office of the land. One prideful African American woman remarked at the conclusion of the Democratic primaries, "This has been the best primary season ever. I had a choice between an African American man and a woman. They were both smart, accomplished, and magnetic. They both addressed issues that were relevant to me and my community. I felt that no matter who ended up getting the nomination, I couldn't lose. It can't get any better for me politically as a Black woman than this."

Would this dual identity group support the candidate who looked like them or would they go with the candidate that they perceived felt their pain and identified and represented the issues that they are most concerned about? In actuality, the support for these two particular candidates may not have had much to do with selecting race over gender or gender over race. Some voted for Senator Clinton because she would become the first female president, just as others voted for Senator Obama because he would become the first African American president, regardless of their stand on the contemporary issues. Political observers could correctly surmise that the hesitation to support either candidate is a reflection of people's views on who the candidates are. Many African American women are looking beyond the layer of race and gender due in large part to the complexities of so many pressing issues currently facing the African American community.

An end to oppression fostered by racism and sexism would bring freedom and a collective exhale to all people, regardless of their race or gender. Are we to rejoice in the nomination of either a woman or an African American as one of our own? African American women have for generations delivered consistent votes for Democratic candidates of various genders and ethnicities. What is the significance of the historic selection of a Black man to be president of the United States? Undoubtedly, the issues of racial and gender inequalities will still remain despite such a remarkable milestone having been reached. The reality is that some did vote for Obama because Clinton is a woman just as some undoubtedly voted for Clinton because Obama is African American. In fact, women of all races and men of color together form an underrepresented plurality of voters in this country. Many voters in the country would ultimately endorse the ideas of a woman or person of color running for president of the United States, just not these particular candidates. The end result was that millions of Americans voted for both candidates in spite of their race and gender.

Both Shirley Chisholm and Carol Moseley Braun have places at the tables of American and African American history. They helped to break the barriers that kept previous generations of both women and women of color from full political representation. The barriers that they tore down opened the path for Barack Obama. Shirley Chisholm made America see that a woman or a man of color could lead this nation when she made her historic and unprecedented run for the presidency in 1972. Carol Moseley Braun did the same by becoming the first African American woman to be elected to the U.S. Senate and incidentally, the seat that she held representing the state of Illinois was later held by Senator Barack Obama. African Americans have feelings of immense pride in the racial symbolism of Obama's election. The struggle for all women, including African American women, to have full representation in national politics continues on.

Chapter 7

Early Indicators of Gender Preference Shift to Racial Preference

This is the most exciting election we've had in such a long time, because you have an African American, an extraordinary man, a person of tremendous talents and abilities, running to become our president; you have a woman running to break the highest and hardest glass ceiling. I don't think either of us wants to inject race or gender in this campaign.

—Senator Hillary Rodham Clinton

When asked on a survey about the choice between presidential candidates Clinton and Obama, one African American woman replied:

I feel the Clinton family did a lot for America. I listen to the Obama campaign and he's a good speaker. I think that Obama would make a Great President someday with more knowledge of how to solve America's problems. And the time will come when America will have both a Black and a Woman as President one day. But at this time, speeches will not get America back on her feet. Right now I feel that Hillary is the best Candidate.[1]

Another African American female Clinton supporter added:

I feel there is so much division between Democrats, that whoever is standing at the end will lose. The people that want the Black man to win and the people who want the woman to win are going to be in for a rude awakening. I feel that the person who loses, that their supporters will go Republican just for spite. I want Hillary to win. I am an African American woman who thinks Clinton has been around long enough to have a lot of experience in the land of the White House, has already fought for medical equality, and helped the uninsured get insurance. If she does not win, I will be voting for McCain. I am voting for the issues not color.[2]

In the 2008 race for the presidency, Senator Hillary Rodham Clinton presented herself as the candidate of experience, using her husband's two terms as president, and her experience as a former first lady and as a second-term junior senator representing the state of New York as confirmation of that experience when she announced on January 27, 2007, her intention to run for the Democratic nomination for president of the United States. Senator Clinton would refer back to the time when she worked at the Yale Child Study Center to work on legal issues involving developmentally disabled children and reminded voters that she had a strong commitment to the Children's Defense Fund.

Many assumed that since Senator Barack Obama emerged as the first African American to win the Iowa caucus, that African Americans would be supporting his candidacy in relatively high numbers. A CNN poll conducted on October 17, 2007, indicated that Senator Hillary Clinton's lead over Senator Obama was growing amongst African American registered Democrats, in particular African American women. Among African American likely Democratic voters, Clinton had a 57-to-30 percent lead over Obama.[3] A number of polls conducted in November 2007 indicated that Senator Clinton had as much as a 15-point lead over Senator Obama among African American women polled.[4] This was an early indication of a possible split amongst African American voters by gender.

Hillary Clinton emerged as the most viable female candidate to ever mount a serious campaign for the presidency. There were other women who had run previous to Clinton, but they were usually heavily underfinanced and could not generate the broad base support necessary to successfully run for the nomination of a major political party. Senator Clinton had some early advantages in the presidential race. Her name recognition was certainly one huge advantage over the freshman senator from Illinois. Another advantage of Senator Clinton's was that she was the assumed frontrunner for the nomination and more people believed at the time that she had the best chance of winning amongst the major contenders in the race. Many voters saw her as a strong contender for the presidency. Clinton had in fact, been touted as a relative shoe-in for the Democratic nomination for months prior to the official start of the presidential campaign season.

Hillary's Negatives

As her campaign progressed, national polls began to show Hillary Clinton's favorable ratings decreasing and her negatives increasing. Some reports indicated that Clinton was eliminated from John Kerry's list of possible vice presidential running mates in 2004 because of the prevailing thought that her high negatives would have hurt the ticket. Fifty-eight percent of Americans said Clinton was not honest and trustworthy, and a record-high 54 percent of Americans had an unfavorable opinion of Clinton, according to a 2008 ABC News/*Washington Post* poll. According to a CBS News/*New York Times* poll dated July 9–17, 2007, 63 percent of those polled said that Clinton was very or somewhat likely to win in November 2008.[5] Sixty-five percent of women polled responded that Clinton would be very or somewhat likely to win in November 2008.[6] When asked if they had a choice between Clinton, Barack Obama, and former senator John Edwards as the Democratic Party nominee, 43 percent of those polled selected Hillary Clinton, 24 percent selected Barack Obama, and 16 percent selected John Edwards.[7]

Apparently, the Clinton White House scandals had taken a significant toll on the perception that many voters had of Senator Clinton, despite the fact that her White House years have been noted as being marked with relative peace and prosperity. The Whitewater scandal as well as her failed national health care initiative remained in the minds of many voters. Some voters found her to be untrustworthy and they were very skeptical of what some perceived to be a potential for a third Clinton administration. Other voters saw her as cold and unemotional. Young voters who were too young to witness her impact during the Clinton years in the White House did not find her candidacy appealing. A significant number of male voters found Clinton unappealing, disliking her image as a strong, domineering woman. It can be difficult for a woman to be viewed as strong and capable and also to be seen as well-liked. Whereas Clinton demonstrates her tenacity to be a strong leader, voters remark that she is viewed as cold and unlikeable. Voters also remarked that she seemed unemotional and unfeeling, hence rendering her a candidate that many voters remained very skeptical about.

The Clinton Dynasty

Perhaps the biggest advantage for the former first lady with the African American electorate was the affinity that many members of the African American community had toward her husband, former president Bill

Clinton. The African American community in Little Rock, Arkansas, inducted him into the Black American Hall of Fame as an honorary member in 2002 to recognize the special relationship that existed between President Clinton and the Black community and for his ongoing efforts on behalf of the Black community both nationally and internationally. The belief remained that African Americans faired quite well economically under the Clinton administration and that resonated with many African American voters. Alan Greenspan, the former chairman of the Federal Reserve for two decades, praises former president Clinton, as he described in his book, of being the president who maintained a consistent, disciplined focus on long-term economic growth. The median household income of African American households came up 21 percent (or $5,104) since 1993, from $24,300 in 1993 to $29,404 in 1998, adjusted for inflation. The real wages of African Americans rose rapidly, up 8.2 percent in the last three years of the Clinton administration. The African American poverty rate declined from 33.1 percent to 26.1 between 1993 and 1998, which was the largest 5-year drop in more than 25 years.[8]

Clinton enjoyed having much influence within the African American electorate. An example of this is during the 2006 U.S. Senate race in the Commonwealth of Virginia; polling place irregularities, including erroneous felon identifications, were being reported throughout the state on election day. The Democratic Party dispatched President Clinton to hit the radio airwaves with a last-minute plea to African American voters in the Commonwealth via Black radio stations to go vote immediately if they had not done so already. Despite having prominent Black leaders in the state such as former Virginia governor Douglas Wilder, Clinton was seen as the one to turn to get the remaining Black voters to the polls that day. Senator Jim Webb, the Democratic candidate, went on to defeat incumbent Republican senator George Allen by a mere 0.5 percentage point.

Bill Clinton had been called the nation's first Black president. Clinton seemed to connect with African Americans in ways in which previous presidents had not. Although Clinton received the ire of many African Americans with his 1996 welfare reform law as well as his foreign policy toward the Rwandan genocide, Clinton's favorability remained high among most African Americans. The Clinton administration became defined by the historic appointments of African Americans to cabinet positions. Clinton appointed more African Americans to cabinet posts than all of the other presidents put together. Fourteen percent of his administration appointees were African American. President Clinton was one of the first

Presidents to appoint African Americans to key positions within his presidential cabinet. Clinton's cabinets consisted of African American secretaries of commerce, agriculture, labor, transportation, energy, and veterans' affairs. Alexis Herman became the first African American to serve as a U.S. secretary of labor. He appointed Jocelyn Elders as the first African American to become the U.S. surgeon general in 1993. Clinton also appointed 14 African Americans as U.S. attorneys and 12 African Americans as U.S. marshals. He also nominated 67 African Americans to the federal bench.

In the 1996 presidential election, 84 percent of African Americans cast their votes for Bill Clinton.[9] President Clinton was also the first president to tour Africa while in office. He touted a record-low African American unemployment rate, reporting that the rate had fallen from 14.2 percent in 1992 to 8 percent in 1999, indicating it to be the lowest rate for African Americans on record.[10] The Clinton administration also took credit for the record high homeownership rate for African Americans. Between the years 1994 and 1999, the number of African American families owning homes increased by 1.1 million. Median income for African American families went up by 21 percent between 1993 and 1999, citing that this was a larger increase than for all Americans.[11]

President Clinton demonstrated a keen interest in Black culture. Following his leaving the White House, President Clinton even set up his offices in New York City's historically Black section of Harlem. He specifically chose that particular neighborhood for the location because he wanted to help revitalize the predominantly African American district. He also remarked that he wanted to use his office in Harlem as a base to fight AIDS and poverty, two huge areas of concern for the African American community. AIDS is currently the number one killer of African American women in the United States and a disproportionate number of African American families live below the poverty line.

Significant numbers of African American and working class voters hoped for the possibility of reinventing the first Clinton presidency through electing Senator Hillary Rodham Clinton president of the United States. Some voters expressed a desire to see the former president back in the White House even as the spouse of the next president. Of course, Clinton detractors were incensed by the notion, and groups and websites were mobilized to mount organized opposition to Senator Clinton's candidacy.

Senator Clinton herself has networked with many traditional civil rights leaders and the congressional Black caucus. The Clintons had an extensive civil rights history in their home state of Arkansas. Senator Clinton even reportedly recommended Lani Guinier to head the Civil Rights Commission as the assistant attorney general for civil rights. When Guinier's perceived radical views became known, her name had to be withdrawn. This was one of the first instances where Black voters began to be skeptical of Clinton loyalty to African Americans, seeing that the president did not vehemently defend Guinier's record and instead asked that her nomination be withdrawn as a result of pressure to nix the controversial nomination.

Senator Clinton did introduce legislation in the Senate to honor Sojourner Truth with a statue in the U.S. Capitol. This legislation that was unanimously approved by the Senate on December 6, 2006, makes Sojourner Truth one of the first African Americans to be honored with a statue in the Capitol. Clinton also introduced legislation to award Dr. Dorothy I. Height, president of the National Council of Negro Women, a congressional medal for her contributions to the country in 2003. Senator Clinton worked to recognize the contributions of other significant African American female heroes to history including Coretta Scott King, Harriet Tubman, Rosa Parks, and Shirley Chisholm.

Clinton's Disadvantages from the Start

Senator Hillary Clinton entered the Democratic presidential nomination race with high negatives and mixed approval ratings.[12] Hillary Clinton seemed to be a somewhat polarizing figure. Senator Clinton's credibility was also questioned by many pundits and voters. Even when she cried publicly, detractors accused her of trying to illicit sympathy from female voters and then accused her of lacking the toughness necessary for the job of president of the United States. There were even some who argued that being married to a former president was no where near the same as an individual's own governing and leadership experience. But also, no former first lady had decided to run for an elective office, much less the presidency of the United States. Hillary Clinton became a trailblazer for women, inadvertently perhaps, by becoming the first first lady in history to seek the office previously held by her husband.

Clinton supporters have argued that the media strongly favored Obama during most of the primary and caucus season. Some pundits would not refer to her as Senator Clinton, but would instead refer to her as Mrs. Clinton. Unfortunately for Hillary Clinton, women seemed to be a little lower on the protectionist pecking order than African Americans. There are some conservative commentators who charged that voters and the mainstream media tended to react quicker toward racist sentiments than to sexist ones.

Clinton had also been accused of not adequately addressing the so-called feminist agenda. She was accused of not fully pushing the core feminist agenda during her presidential campaign. The accusers wanted Clinton to declare herself as the female candidate and put feminist issues at the top of her campaign platform. Clinton herself claimed that if you looked up the word feminist in the dictionary that you would be likely to find her name: "If you look in the dictionary, the word feminist means someone who believes in equal rights for women in society, in the economy, the political process—generally believes in the equality of women. And I certainly believe in the equality of women."[13] Clinton's campaign attempted from the very beginning to prevent her from being labeled the female candidate since it would be critical for her not to turn off male supporters. This was seen as a negative, given the electorate's questions about a female's capability of becoming commander-in-chief, since the country had never had a female president.

Elizabeth Edwards, then wife of former North Carolina Senator and 2008 presidential candidate John Edwards, charged that Clinton was too quiet on feminist issues. As noted by Michael McAuliffe, in a *New York Daily News* article on July 18, 2007, although Edwards was sympathetic to Clinton's predicament, "You want to reassure them you're as good as a man. And sometimes you feel you have to behave as a man and not talk about women's issues," Edwards said.[14] The Clinton campaign approach it seemed from the beginning to be seen as being strong enough to be commander-in-chief and not to run as the female candidate. Female groups felt that as the first viable female presidential candidate in history that it was her responsibility to make gender a centerpiece of her campaign. Some feminist groups such as NARAL Pro-Choice America chose instead to endorse candidate Barack Obama. Clinton may have lost some crucial early support from some female and younger voters who would have been galvanized by a stronger focus on feminist issues.

Geraldine Ferraro, a staunch Clinton ally and women's issues advocate, stated the importance of electing Clinton as the first female president: "It's been 23 years since I was the first woman on a major party presidential slate, and I remember what it was like breaking that barrier—including the barrage of attacks at the hands of the Republicans," Ferraro wrote. "Now

Hillary is poised to break the biggest glass ceiling of them all. This time, when we elect the best, most qualified candidate for president, for the first time we'll be putting a woman in the White House."

Most national polls conducted in the beginning of the presidential campaign season indicated that when women were surveyed as a group, Hispanics and other ethnicities favored Hillary Clinton while most African American women favored Barack Obama. In the latter part of her presidential campaign, detractors accused Clinton of using her gender card to the maximum. Clinton was advised to show the voters in New Hampshire her vulnerability and her softer side. Clinton cried one morning while at a campaign stop at a coffee shop in New Hampshire. It seemed to make her more appealing, particularly to a demographic of older, female voters. Some say sisterhood was activated that day by Hillary Clinton displaying her more vulnerable side. Although it initially helped Clinton with some voters, in the final analysis, she was beaten by a candidate who outfinanced and outcampaigned her.

Age Divisions among African American Women

Early polling revealed that 45 percent of young female voters surveyed between the ages of 18 and 29 were split evenly between who they viewed most favorably, Clinton or Obama.[15] Clinton was viewed more favorably by African American women by a whopping 77 percent.[16] Older Blacks, primarily Black women, viewed Senator Clinton as being more electable than Senator Obama. Many responded through polling that they believed that Clinton had the track record of working toward issues important to them. Black women regarded Senator Clinton as a strong health care advocate. Many older women expressed reservations that America was ready for an African American president. Some younger women may not be as familiar with Hillary Clinton when she was first lady of Arkansas or of her years in the White House. It was also theorized that younger women who may not have found it as imperative as older women to vote for a female for president because they are too young to have yet been adversely affected by feminist issues such as job discrimination. Hillary Clinton attempted to attract swing voters who were African American women. There were numbers of prominent Black women such as poet Maya Angelou and Congresswoman Sheila Jackson Lee of Texas who would make ads and public appearances on behalf of Senator Clinton. These measures did have a positive effect until Obama's eventual surge in the polls.

Some African Americans expressed reservations at supporting a candidate such as Obama who had such sparse credentials. Many argued that this was actually an advantage for Obama because he was not seen as part of the Washington elite, while Clinton was viewed as the continuation of the Clinton political dynasty. Perhaps the idea of having a Bush or a Clinton in the Oval Office for 20 consecutive years was not desirous to the American public.

Clinton's finished third in the Iowa caucus. Barack Obama became the first African American to win the caucus. Obama spent more money in the state, assisting in his caucus victory. It was originally anticipated that women would give most of their support to Clinton but in the end they ended up splitting their vote between Clinton and Obama. It most definitely would have been a much different nomination contest overall had Hillary been able to pull out a win in the Iowa caucus.

Senator Clinton seemed to become more competitive when John Edwards dropped out of the race for it seemed as though Edwards helped to split Clinton's base. Perhaps if John Edwards had taken more from Obama than Clinton, her chances of winning the nomination may have seemed been better. It is quite easy to conclude that in the political climate of the 2008 presidential election, the thirst for change may have begun to trump both Clinton's experience and name recognition advantage.

Chapter 8

The Consequential Shift to Obama

Race is still a powerful force in this country. Any African American candidate, or any Latino candidate, or Asian candidate or woman candidate confronts a higher threshold in establishing himself to the voters. . . . Are some voters not going to vote for me because I'm African American? Those are the same voters who probably wouldn't vote for me because of my politics.

—Senator Barack Obama

Senator Barack Obama's victory in the Iowa caucus on January 3, 2008 was the beginning of a modern-day phenomenon in American politics. Senator Hillary Clinton was the presumed frontrunner for the Democratic nomination for president of the United States. Many thought the relatively unknown junior senator from Illinois to be unelectable. He was relatively unknown to the national stage and had not even finished a full term as a senator representing the state of Illinois.

The Speech

Senator Obama was introduced to the American electorate at the 2004 Democratic National Convention. There, he delivered an extraordinary speech that moved millions of viewers across the country as well as the attendees to the convention. There were numerous variables that made Obama a great selection to deliver the keynote address at the convention. Obama was powerfully charismatic and articulate. This made for a huge appeal toward younger voters. Senate politics played a role also. With Democrats needing to pick up just two seats to gain control of the

Senate, Barack Obama's campaign was crucial because a Republican-held seat, Peter Fitzgerald's in Illinois, was up for grabs.

Democratic party insiders hoped that the national exposure would energize Obama's Illinois campaign for the Senate.[1]

That amazing speech launched Barack Obama into national prominence. Historians will most likely cite that speech as key in the establishment of Senator Obama as a potential candidate for president in 2008. U.S. Representative Barbara Jordan, the first Black woman to deliver a keynote address at a Democratic National Convention, also wowed the nation in 1976 with a stirring speech of her own that many historians noted as one of the best in convention history.[2] Senator Obama would go on to win the Illinois Senate race that same year, becoming the only African American member of the U.S. Senate at the time. The debate lingered as to whether or not the country would be prepared though to elect an African American president for the first time in its history.

In February 2007, Senator Obama announced his intention to run for the Democratic nomination for president in Springfield, Illinois, symbolically linking his announcement to the legacy of President Abraham Lincoln. Two months before the first electoral contests in the Iowa caucus and New Hampshire primary, national opinion polls showed him trailing behind Senator Hillary Clinton.

Obama's presidential campaign began raising record amounts of money from its onset. The Obama campaign raised $58 million during the first six months of 2007, topping all of the other candidates and exceeding previously set records for the first six-month time period of any year before an election year.[3] Money from small donors, donors who contributed in amounts of less than $200, accounted for $16.4 million of Obama's history-making total, more than any other Democratic presidential candidate.[4] In January 2008, Obama's campaign raised $36.8 million, the most ever raised in one month by a presidential candidate in Democratic Party primaries and caucuses.[5]

Racial Consciousness

Racial consciousness has a rather undefined impact upon the political attitudes of many African American women. Many African American voters perceived the Clintons as using racial divisiveness as a campaign weapon against Senator Obama, and indirectly, the African American electorate during Hillary Clinton's presidential campaign. African American voters resented the suggestion that exploitation of race and class fears were being promoted to stir resentment and bitterness for political gain.

Former vice presidential candidate Geraldine Ferraro suggested that Obama was winning because of the color of his skin. Surprisingly so voters were quietly agreeing with Ferraro's premise. One African American female supporter of Senator Clinton agreed: "With 90 percent of African American voters opting for Obama and the media are silent on the racist issue! If 90 percent of female voters opted for Clinton, the press would go crazy on the gender issue. Is this a double standard I ask? This should be pointed out to the media or better still to female voters in this election."[6]

Gov. Ed Rendell, one of Hillary Clinton's most visible supporters, hinted that some White Pennsylvania voters were likely to vote against Senator Clinton's rival Barack Obama because he is African American. "You've got conservative Whites here, and I think there are some Whites who are probably not ready to vote for an African American candidate,"[7] Rendell said during the campaign.

Some Black voters were apprehensive about supporting Senator Obama as he was relatively new to the national stage. Once Obama was able to win in Iowa, a predominantly White-populated state, many began to reconsider his ability to get elected despite what they considered to be a lack of national experience. Leading Black magazines began putting Obama on their covers such as was the case with *Ebony* magazine, whose headline read, "In Our Lifetime." African Americans began to dream and then they began to believe. They began to seriously envision the possibility of a man of color becoming president of the United States. Slowly but surely the tide began changing—in Obama's favor.

The Oprah Effect

In South Carolina, Hillary Clinton held a slight lead over Obama according to polls taken in late 2007, but a *Los Angeles Times*/Bloomberg poll of likely Democratic voters showed Senator Clinton having an early wide lead in the state. In comes icon Oprah Winfrey onboard the Obama campaign. Winfrey, the most powerful African American woman in the country and one of the most powerful and influential women in the world, campaigned for Obama early in the presidential primary season. She made campaign appearances in the states of Iowa, New Hampshire, and South Carolina, making the most campaign appearances in the latter state. During one campaign appearance in Cedar Rapids, Iowa, Winfrey made these remarks in regards to the candidacy of Senator Obama: "I've never taken this kind of risk before nor felt compelled to stand up and speak out before because there wasn't anyone to stand up and speak up for," Winfrey told thousands of people in Cedar Rapids Saturday evening. "We need a president who can bring us all together," she said. "I know [Barack Obama] is the one."[8]

Oprah also made campaign appearances in California where she held a fundraiser for Obama at her Santa Barbara estate in September 2007, where she raised approximately $3 million for his presidential campaign.[9] It was the first time that Ms. Winfrey had chosen to endorse and throw her powerful brand behind a political candidate. Her support gave Obama unadulterated access to a media empire. Obama benefited from appearances on Oprah Winfrey's high-profile talk show and having the world's most famous media star make appearances on his behalf on the campaign trail. Because Oprah's appeal cuts across so many demographic groups—Black, White, wealthy, middle income, urban, suburban—her endorsement was significant to his campaign. Winfrey's endorsement also helped to fortify trust among White, middle-aged, and middle class voters. Viewers of her show were extremely loyal to Oprah so if she endorsed a candidate, those potential voters would be more likely to vote for the candidate(s) endorsed by Oprah Winfrey. She had seen for herself Barack Obama's amazing rise to political stardom and all that he had accomplished in Chicago as a young community organizer, and then as a state legislator, and she was willing to vouch for that. Oprah's impact helped Obama in some areas that would be crucial in his bid to win the nomination. Oprah helped to build trust among African Americans for Senator Obama. According to a 2007 *Washington Post*/ABC News poll, Winfrey's outreach would be the most successful among African Americans. Sixteen percent of African Americans polled said they were more likely to support Obama as a result of her endorsement and the figure among African American women was 19 percent.[10]

Oprah helped to take women voters away from Clinton in numerous states, including in the state of South Carolina where most of the Democratic electorate there is African American. One of the results was that large numbers of African American women shifted toward Obama. One of Obama's initial problems with African American voters was their unfamiliarity with him and his lack of name recognition nationally. Many African Americans simply did not know much about Senator Obama and what his campaign was all about. It was Oprah's charge to bring out these voters who may not have heard him before and what his message was. Winfrey drew thousands of voters to arenas in Iowa, New Hampshire, and South Carolina. People were drawn to see Oprah and were available to hear Obama speak, providing a fantastic opportunity for him to speak to voters who might not otherwise come out to hear a politician speak. When the opponent is a woman, having one of the most popular women in the country endorse your candidacy is politically expedient. It was a huge asset to have the most powerful African American woman in history influence African American female voters who make up a significant part of the Democratic Party electorate.

Michelle Obama and African American Women

There were African Americans who challenged the validity of Obama's Blackness, due in part to Obama being biracial, the product of a White mother and a Black Kenyan father. Also, African Americans were quite ambivalent about this newcomer to the national stage who they knew so relatively little about. Bring in Senator Obama's wife, Michelle Obama, who many feel helped to authenticate his Blackness. Mrs. Obama grew up in a middle-class area of Chicago and is the descendant of former American slaves.

Michelle Robinson Obama is a graduate of Princeton University and Harvard Law School. Her intellect and ability to speak publicly and connect with audiences made her a natural to hit the campaign trail in support of her husband's candidacy. In 2007, Michelle began to give stump speeches for her husband's presidential campaign at various locations throughout the United States. Early in the campaign, voters were mesmerized by her humor and crowds responded well to anecdotes that she shared about her family life. She came across as smart and likeable. Mrs. Obama spoke on issues important to many voters, particularly working women and African Americans, with passion and zeal, moving thousands of voters to take another look at her husband's candidacy. She talked about being a working mother and having difficulty paying her student loans. Many women felt that they could relate to her and that she understood and cared about their primary concerns as voters. She was seen to have been an excellent surrogate to help attract women voters to her husband's campaign.

When Michelle Obama was sent out on the campaign trail, the campaign made a major strategic move to lure African American female voters by doing this. Mrs. Obama spoke on issues that struck a chord with African American voters including race, education, and motherhood. She also spoke of the fears that many had that her husband may get shot and helped ease the fears of many by sharing how she cast away her own fears for her husband's safety. Mrs. Obama also campaigned separately from her husband, impressing crowds with her down-to-earth charm, her strong support of her family, and her sharp and engaging articulation of the issues. Voters liked Michelle Obama's image as a supportive wife and loving mother. She talked about the struggles early on in their marriage and how difficult it was when her husband was never home with her and the children because he was working or campaigning. She talked about her middle class childhood growing up in Chicago. She came from humble beginnings to become a well-respected attorney in her own right. She served as a shining example to Black women everywhere and Black women responded with much enthusiasm for Barack Obama's candidacy.

Many argued that Senator Obama's wife strengthened his racial authenticity. There are those who distinguish Obama because he is not the direct descendant of slaves, as most African Americans are in this country. "She gives credence to his blackness," one voter remarked. "If he hadn't married a strong, Black woman I don't know if I would have supported him."[11]

The Fear Factor

Voters connected the fear of assassination to doubts regarding his electability and maintained a level of skepticism about an Obama presidential candidacy. Many African Americans stated that they feared that someone or some entity would do something to harm Senator Obama or his family. Obama received Secret Service protection in May 2007, the earliest that any presidential candidate has ever been granted protection during a presidential campaign season. At that time, Obama had at least a dozen Secret Service agents at his disposal. The practice of granting presidential candidates with Secret Service protection began following the assassination of Robert F. Kennedy in 1968. Those who lived through the turmoil of the 1960s are particularly concerned about his safety. Fears about Obama's safety transcend racial lines. White Americans have similar fears for Obama, particularly for those who say that he evokes memories of the late president John F. Kennedy.[12]

Obama himself has played down such fears concerning his safety. Michelle Obama has stated that she does not share the same fears as others. Despite those fears, she remarks that she feels strongly that Barack is so special, that he has to be shared with the world. Those fears cannot stop their mission. Mrs. Obama's speaking on the sensitive topic in interviews and on the campaign trail alleviated the fears of many voters, many of whom were African American.

The Shift

Various polls conducted in January 2007 indicated that Senator Hillary Clinton was beginning to lose a significant amount of support among African American likely voters. The polls indicated that the majority of African American registered Democrats began to support Senator Obama. A nationwide survey conducted by CNN/Opinion Research Corporation showed that 59 percent of African American Democrats responded that they now supported Obama as opposed to 31 percent who were still supporting Senator Clinton.[13] The 28-point shift towards Senator Obama is a reversal from October 2007 when Clinton was leading in some polls by 24 points. Hillary Clinton's sizable margin over Obama had been cut in half in large part due to the growing support for Obama from African American voters.[14] The gender breakdown shows that 81 percent of Black female voters and 86 percent of Black male voters went for Obama, averaging out to 83 percent, with African American women making up a larger share of the African American electorate.

Respected African American religious leaders such as Reverend Joseph Lowery and Reverend Jesse Jackson united to voice support for Senator Obama. Many carefully displayed support through a delicate balancing act of encouraging increased voter registration and participation and support for the candidate who would go on to become the first African American president of the United States.

Many never envisioned that an African American man would ever come this close to the presidency of the United States. That revelation had a dramatic impact on African American voters who began to believe that Obama *could* win. Once Obama won Iowa's first in the nation presidential caucuses, there began to be a shift in support for his candidacy. Black America began to believe in and vote for Obama in primaries and caucuses throughout the nation in significant numbers. Increased exposure to Senator Obama increased his favorable rating within the African

American electorate as well as his name recognition. One example, in the Indiana primary, Obama won large numbers of votes in towns such as Gary and Indianapolis, which coincidentally have larger numbers of African American voters.

A poll conducted by CNN/Opinion Research found that more Americans were more prepared for an African American president than a female president. The poll showed that 72 percent of Whites and 61 percent of Blacks believed that the country was ready for a Black president.[15] When asked if the country was ready for a female president, both groups were less certain. Sixty-three percent of Whites and Blacks thought that the country was ready for a woman as president.[16] That percent was up for Whites but down among Blacks since December 2006. "Black president" may have meant "Barack Obama" to those polled, and "female president" may have meant "Hillary Clinton," and the poll may actually have been saying that the country was more ready for Barack Obama than Hillary Clinton. Whereas Obama's message appealed to a significant part of the Democratic Party electorate, for many, Hillary Clinton represented the Washington establishment. The impact of Obama's likeability and charismatic persona proved to be a huge asset to him, major factors that proved to be difficult for the Clinton campaign to overcome. Many Black Americans took notice when Obama began to gain momentum. The transfer of African American votes from Clinton to Obama sealed the nomination for Obama.

It has been suggested that African American women are African American first and women second as perhaps demonstrated through the voting trends of this demographic during the 2008 Democratic primaries. Others have charged that Hillary Clinton lost because sexism in this country is more difficult to overcome than racism. Senator Obama was extremely successful at peeling away at portions of Clinton's core electorate, including African American women. Senator Obama's message resonated with millions of voters of various races despite his racial lineage. He was able to win in states such as Vermont where there are fewer African American voters. African American women collectively, many of whom are mothers, feel that it sends a tremendous message to children of color to have an African American elected president of the United States. When accepting the nomination as his party's presidential nominee, Senator Obama said, "Tonight, we mark the end of one historic journey with the beginning of another."[17] Obama offered hope and improved opportunities to many voters who believed in his candidacy. Obama's vision for the country and his effective campaign strategy won over millions of voters, many of whom were African American, thus making it possible for him to become the first African American presidential nominee of any major political party in the United States.

Chapter 9

The Historic 2008 Democratic Primaries and Caucuses

We are choosing hope over fear, we are choosing unity over division and sending a powerful message that change is coming to America.

—Senator Barack Obama

To secure the Democratic presidential nomination in the 2008 presidential election cycle, a candidate had to secure at least 2,117 votes from delegates, which was a simple majority of the 4,233 designated delegate vote total. Delegates would then be charged with deciding who the party presidential nominee would be at the Democratic national convention in Denver, Colorado, in August 2008. Candidates from both parties competed in numerous state caucuses and primaries. The result of these contests would determine the number of pledged delegates who would commit to vote for a particular candidate during the party's national convention. Delegates were selected from 48 states, including the District of Columbia, and Puerto Rico. Florida and Michigan had half a vote each. Rules were set up by the Democratic Party in early 2007 to prevent states from moving their primaries or caucuses earlier in the party nomination schedule. The designated penalty for states who violated this established rule would be to shut them out from participation at the party's national convention. Florida and Michigan were charged with violating party rules by holding their primaries too early in the nominating cycle. (Senator Clinton would go on to win both the Florida and Michigan Democratic party primaries.)

Democratic primaries and caucuses are the means through which candidates are nominated for president in the Democratic Party. A primary is an election where voters actually go to the polls to cast votes for candidates for the party presidential nomination. Party delegates are then selected to represent candidates at the national party convention based upon the results of both the primaries and caucuses. A caucus is a process where registered voters of specific communities meet to discuss candidates and party platforms. In caucuses such as in Iowa, for example, a candidate must get 15 percent of the caucus votes, which is considered minimum support for viability. The Iowa caucus is the first in the nation to occur during a presidential election cycle.

Pledged delegates are typically allocated to each of the 50 states based on the proportion of votes each state gave to the Democratic candidate in the prior three presidential elections as well as the percentage of votes from the state's allotment in the Electoral College.[1] The 2008 Democratic National Convention convened that year in Denver.

Between November 2006 and February 2007, eight major candidates announced their intentions to run for the Democratic presidential nomination. These individuals included the former first lady Hillary Rodham Clinton, Illinois senator Barack Obama, Delaware senator Joe Biden, Iowa governor Tom Vilsack, Vermont senator Chris Dodd, former Democratic party vice presidential candidate John Edwards, Congressman Dennis Kucinich of Ohio, and New Mexico governor Bill Richardson. In the first three months of 2007, Clinton and Obama raised more than $20 million each and Edwards raised more than $12 million. The three candidates quickly became the frontrunners for the nomination, a status they held all the way through the end of 2007.[2] In December 2007, Clinton was leading in the number of superdelegates, and was leading in national polling by an almost two-to-one margin over both Obama and John Edwards.

The Iowa Caucus

Democratic Party caucuses are usually closed meetings of members of the party at the local or state level where delegates to the party's national convention are selected.

Following the established tradition, the 2008 primary season began with the Iowa caucus on January 3, 2008. The Iowa caucus generally draws a lot of national attention. It is the first contest for both the Democratic and Republican parties in the process to nominate candidates to run for the presidency from the party. Iowa has an overwhelming White and elderly population. For most of the year, Senator Obama trailed behind several other candidates in polling. Obama counted on independents and young voters to participate in the caucuses. Obama's strategy worked. Obama won the Iowa caucus with 38 percent of the vote, over Edwards, 30 percent, and Clinton, 29 percent. He won among Democrats and independents with some help from Republicans who crossed over to participate in the Democratic caucus. Obama won more of the female vote as well, despite running against the most viable female presidential candidate in U.S. history. His victory brought him to national prominence as many voters began to become engaged in the race for the first time.

After Obama's upset win in Iowa, the prevailing thought was that he would ride a wave of momentum through the New Hampshire primary and then he would go on to win the Democratic nomination. Observers began to suggest that Clinton's campaign would be coming to an end as Obama surged to a 10-point lead in the New Hampshire polls. However, the race turned quickly in the days before the primary, and the polls were slow to indicate a surge in Clinton's direction.

The New Hampshire Primary

A state primary election is a preliminary election where voters can cast votes to nominate candidates from their party for elective office. There is a state law that mandates that New Hampshire be the first state to hold their presidential primary during the presidential election cycle. The legal statute reads:

> The presidential primary election shall be held on the second Tuesday in March or on a date selected by the secretary of state which is 7 days or more immediately preceding the date on which any other state shall hold a similar election, whichever is earlier, of each year when a president of the United States is to be elected or the year previous. Said primary shall be held in connection with the regular March town meeting or election or, if held on any other day, at a special election called by the secretary of state for that purpose.[3]

The morning before the 2008 New Hampshire primary, Hillary Clinton responded very emotionally to a friendly question from a voter at a town hall meeting. Footage of the moment was replayed on television stations throughout the day, accompanied by commentaries that went from sympathetic support to indignant outrage. Voters, however, rallied to Clinton's defense, and she ended up winning a surprising three-point victory over Obama in the primary's popular vote. Clinton and Obama tied in the final delegate count. The New Hampshire primary caught everyone by surprise. Some analysts suggested that the polls had been so wrong beforehand in part because voters in the overwhelmingly White state had been reluctant to share their true, race-based reservations about Senator Obama. The New Hampshire primary was held on January 8, 2008, and voting in both parties drew a record 529,542 votes from both major parties, breaking the previous record by 25 percent. Hillary Clinton ended up winning the New Hampshire Democratic primary with 39 percent of the popular vote and earning nine delegates with Barack Obama getting 36 percent of the popular vote and nine delegates as well.

The South Carolina Primary

The 2008 South Carolina Democratic presidential primary took place on January 26, 2008. Historically, as far back as 1914, it is estimated that there were 100,000 more Blacks than Whites in South Carolina, and that Black women were the largest group of voters. By at least one estimate, Black women could make up as much as 30 percent of the South Carolina vote in the South Carolina Primary.[4] Senator Barack Obama of Illinois won the primary's popular vote by a 29 percent margin. This would be the first primary to feature a large proportion of African Americans within the Democratic electorate. Already behind in some of the state polls, Hillary Clinton left South Carolina to campaign in some of the Super Tuesday states, former president Bill Clinton, stayed behind in South Carolina and engaged in a series of heated exchanges with Obama. CBS News reported, "By injecting himself into the Democratic primary campaign with a series of inflammatory and negative statements, Bill Clinton may have helped his wife's presidential hopes in the long term but at the cost of his reputation with a group of voters African Americans that have long been one of his strongest bases of political support."[5] Obama went on to win the state by a more than two-to-one margin over Clinton. Obama received 55 percent of the vote to Clinton's 27 percent and Edwards's 18 percent.[6] South Carolina was significant because it was the first primary contest in a Southern state and the first primary in a state in which African Americans make up a sizable percentage of the electorate for the Democratic Party. For Democrats, it was also the last primary before 22 states hosted their primaries or caucuses on Super Tuesday.

In the critical South Carolina primary, Senator Obama won over both men and women. African Americans represented 55 percent of the

Democratic electorate in that state. African American women represent about 3 in 10 primary voters there. In South Carolina, Obama aimed to siphon off some of Clinton's core supporters—women—making African American women key players in the contest.[7] Claims of race-baiting apparently pushed significant numbers of African American voters to the Obama camp where they stayed for the rest of the primary contests.

Donna Brazile, former national campaign manager to former Vice President Al Gore, predicted that African American women would decide who would win and who would lose the South Carolina Democratic primary. There are those that use the results of primary contests like the 2008 South Carolina primary to theorize that in the world of presidential politics, race trumps gender. It at times appears that young, White voters are more willing to vote for a Black candidate than young, Black voters are willing to vote for a White candidate. Some analysis of the statistics found that young White voters seemed to perceive race as less of a factor in their voting preferences, since more than half of them selected Mr. Obama. More than 90 percent of Blacks voted for Mr. Obama, creating a large racial bloc. Female Black voters preferred Senator Obama by essentially the same margin as male Black voters.[8]

On the day of the South Carolina primary, Bill Clinton is quoted as saying, "Jesse Jackson won South Carolina in '84 and '88. Jackson ran a good campaign. And Obama ran a good campaign here."[9] Clinton was comparing Obama's expected win to Jesse Jackson's victory in the 1988 South Carolina primary. Clinton's comments were harshly criticized. He was accused of attempting to dismiss the eventual primary results and marginalize Obama by making a subliminal implication that he was the Black candidate. Obama's momentum from his win in South Carolina was lessened somewhat by Clinton's win in Florida the next week.

Former senator John Edwards suspended his candidacy for the Democratic nomination on January 30, 2008. He did not immediately endorse either of the two frontrunners. Neither Clinton nor Obama had a clear lead heading into the all-important Super Tuesday primaries. Super Tuesday involved some 23 states and territories and more than 1,600 delegates up for grabs.

Super Tuesday

Senators Clinton and Obama traded victories in the Super Tuesday contests on February 5, 2008. Twenty-two states, including the American Samoa, conducted primaries or caucuses on Super Tuesday. Senator Obama won Alabama, Alaska, Colorado, Connecticut, Delaware, Georgia, Idaho, Illinois, Kansas, Minnesota, Missouri, North Dakota, and Utah. Senator Clinton won the states of Arizona, Arkansas, California, Massachusetts, New Jersey, New Mexico, New York, Oklahoma, Tennessee, and American Samoa.

Clinton and Obama essentially came out even following the Super Tuesday contests, giving Obama even more momentum going into the February primaries. Following the Super Tuesday primaries, Senator Clinton announced that she had loaned her campaign $5 million. Obama announced that he had raised a record $32 million in January, much of this coming from new contributors.[10] Clinton's supporters helped the Clinton campaign raise $6 million online in just 36 hours.[11] The Obama campaigned announced shortly thereafter that they had raised $7.5 million in 36 hours.[12]

Clinton scored big wins in the states of Ohio and Rhode Island. She won the Texas primary, but lost the Texas caucus. Obama's campaign focused on staying as close to Clinton in the delegate count as possible. Obama went on to win the total delegate count in the state of Texas, and he stayed close to Clinton in Ohio. After winning contests in Wyoming and Mississippi, Obama quickly erased Clinton's recent campaign victories.

As the race moved on to other large and important delegate-rich states, some observers began to predict that they believed Clinton had little chance to overcome Obama's lead in pledged delegates. Some suggested that if Clinton could put enough doubts out there regarding Obama's electability, she could stop his momentum. Another suggested strategy was to advocate for the Michigan and Florida delegates to be seated at the convention. Perhaps if she could convince the superdelegates to support her then she could still get the nomination. Clinton was running out of time, and Speaker of the House Nancy Pelosi, also the chairwoman of the 2008 Democratic National Convention, publicly stated that it would be harmful to the party if superdelegates ended up overturning the pledged delegate vote.

On April 22, Clinton scored won a big primary victory by winning the coveted Pennsylvania primary. Obama then won the North Carolina primary on May 6 by almost 15 percentage points, energized by the large African American electorate in the state. The win in North Carolina for Obama effectively erased Clinton's gain in winning the Pennsylvania primary. Clinton won the Indiana primary by a mere percentage point. By this time, Obama led by 164 pledged delegates. There were only 217 pledged delegates left to be decided in the remaining contests. Observers began declaring that the race was over. Obama gave an election night speech that looked forward to the general election campaign against McCain. The pace of superdelegate endorsements began to increase. By May 10, Obama's superdelegate total had surpassed Clinton's for the first time in the nomination race.

On June 3, the day of the final primaries in South Dakota and Montana, Obama received approximately 60 superdelegate endorsements. By evening, major new outlets announced Obama as the winner of the Democratic presidential nomination as the superdelegate endorsements put him past the 2,117 delegate total necessary to clinch the party's nomination. Obama was then clear to claim the title of presumptive Democratic presidential nominee in a victory speech in St. Paul, Minnesota.

On June 7, 2008, Senator Hillary Clinton conceded the Democratic nomination to Senator Barack Obama at the National Building Museum in Washington, DC, by suspending her campaign and endorsing Senator Obama. Senator Clinton inspired millions of Americans through her monumental campaign. She registered thousands of new voters and garnered the most votes of any female candidate in history. The legacy of her historic and groundbreaking campaign will be of a trailblazer for the day when a woman will surely be elected president of the United States. Thanks in large part to the candidacy of Hillary Clinton, we can now see how close we really are.

The 2008 Democratic Party primaries and caucuses produced historic and unprecedented levels of voter turnout. From January 3 through February 5, Democratic turnout exceeded Republican turnout, 19.1 million to 13.1 million.[13] The record Democratic turnout was attributed mainly to voter exuberance over the first viable African American and female candidates for the Democratic nomination for president, discontent over the Iraq War, and a highly contested primary race.

Where Did the Clinton Campaign Go Wrong?

Senator Hillary Clinton had numerous prominent African American women such as Sheila Jackson Lee, Congresswoman from Texas and the late Stephanie Tubbs Jones, Congresswoman from Ohio, tour states throughout the country on her behalf. These women also held public forums with her and provided introductions to her at campaign rallies. These prominent African American women included legendary poet and author Maya Angelou. Once Obama got ahead of Clinton in the number of delegates, his lead was something that she could never overcome. Clinton's advisors assumed that the nomination would be decided by Super Tuesday. On Super Tuesday, he emerged with 20 more delegates than Clinton. After Super Tuesday, Obama won the 11 remaining February primaries and caucuses, 10 of them were consecutive wins. An overwhelming majority of Black women voted for Obama with 96 percent of the vote compared to Black men at 95 percent.

Obama's recruitment of younger voters and a base of activist voters gave him some big advantages.[14] Grassroots mobilization efforts in some of the states that may have been overlooked by Clinton also gave his campaign a big advantage.[15] The youth vote turned out heavily for Obama in the state of Iowa. This demographic was critical in pushing Obama to victory in that state. That first victory in the Iowa caucus caught the nation's attention and helped to propel Obama into his eventual frontrunner status. People slowly began to believe that he could win and they began to vote for him in larger numbers.

The Clinton Machine from the Past

Hillary Clinton relied heavily on people that were part of the inner circle from President Clinton's 1992 and 1996 campaigns as well as some longtime staffers from her days as First Lady. Critics charge that the political landscape has changed and that her advisors did not catch up with the changes. They were accused of being out of touch and relying on the perception of the huge popularity of the Clinton brand. The Clinton machine was supposed to deliver in terms of money, organization, and votes. It did all of those things, but Obama was able to create his own powerful machine from grassroots organizations. Clinton's machine looked old and slow in comparison.

Clinton has been, above all else, a victim of timing. What some decreed as her time overlapped with Obama's and she came up short. But for Obama's candidacy, Clinton would surely be the Democratic nominee and quite possibly the next president of the United States. Clinton entered the presidential race as the frontrunner with a strategy that attempted to incorporate positioning for a general election campaign. Once her campaign was thrown off that track by the Iowa caucus loss, she was unable to come up with a comprehensive alternative.

Clearly, to some, her greatest blunder was to attempt to marginalize Obama by casting him as "the Black candidate." By so doing, she helped turn his weak support among Black voters into a huge advantage, which, in and of itself was not going to win him the nomination, but it did assure that the only way she could beat him is by winning the numbers game. No matter how successful she has been or may yet be in revealing possible Obama weaknesses in the general election, the superdelegates were not going to take the nomination from him and give it to her. To do so would risk permanently alienating a key constituency of the party, Black voters, and risk defeat in the November general election.

In the final analysis, however, it may not be so much what the Clinton campaign did wrong, but what the Obama campaign did correctly. Despite the prevailing thought, the nomination was never Clinton's to lose. Obama ended up getting 78 percent of the African American vote, which fueled his victory. This was an example of the African American voting bloc having a direct impact on the election of Barack Obama as president of the United States. Edwards and Clinton ended up splitting the White vote, which resulted in Obama's 55 percent to 27 percent win over Clinton. It turned out to be the largest victory of the first four Democratic primary contests. At the end of 2007, Hillary Clinton had almost $38 million cash on hand.[16] Included in this amount was $10 million from her Senate campaign fund. Clinton's campaign rapidly began to run out of money and her campaign would at the end of the campaign cycle be over $20 million in the red. This was a critical development in the campaign for Clinton. This was only the second consecutive election cycle where the candidate who raised the most money heading into the nominating contests would not be the nominee.

Senator Hillary Clinton of New York, Barack Obama's chief opponent for the 2008 Democratic presidential nomination, won more of the larger populated states. These were states that allocated Clinton 1,835.5 delegates, more than the 1,574 selected in states Obama won.[17] The outcome would be have been different if the party awarded delegates to the convention on a winner-take-all basis. In the Democratic Party system, any candidate who achieves 15 percent support in a state's primary or caucus will get a share of that state or territory's delegates, and each candidate's overall number of delegates will determine their share of the vote. In a winner-take-all system Clinton would have gotten almost 700 delegates from those wins.[18]

Obama stayed close in the states he lost while getting big wins in numerous primaries. An example of the power and influence of the African

American electorate was its strong showing in the city of Atlanta where it, along with a strong showing among White Atlanta suburbanites, had a noted impact on the 2008 Democratic presidential primary in the state of Georgia. Obama won Georgia by more than 35 points. He received 33 more delegates than Clinton received.[19] By winning Illinois and Georgia, Obama received 88 more delegates than Clinton, thus eradicating her wins in huge delegate-rich states New York and California.[20] The other Super Tuesday primaries went in Clinton's favor. Obama ended up winning every caucus except for the one in American Samoa.[21]

The story of the Democratic presidential race of 2008 may be the decision by the Clinton campaign to run noncompetitive campaigns in some Super Tuesday caucus states, due to Clinton's lack of cash flow. This allowed the Obama campaign to run up his delegate totals. Obama's lead became insurmountable following Super Tuesday. Clinton was ill-financed and unprepared to continue her campaign past Super Tuesday.

Ideally, presidential primaries should be about putting the best candidate forward to represent the ideals and vision of a political party. Each candidate played his or her cards well—objective factors and the sequence of key events simply gave Obama a better hand and doomed Clinton. Obama's ability to win big in little states and lose little in big states served his campaign strategy quite successfully.

Hillary Clinton was the first woman, regardless of race to be taken seriously as a candidate for president of the United States from a major political party. At one point in the Democratic presidential nomination contest, it came down to the rubric of change versus experience. Former presidential candidate John Edwards also touted that he could bring forth the mantra of change for the nation. Voters would go on to convincingly support the candidacy of Barack Obama for the presidency of the United States.

Hillary brought experience, voter familiarity, and the good memories of the Clinton years with her to the campaign table when she announced her candidacy for the Democratic nomination for president of the United States. She came into the race with some high negatives, and voters questioning her likeability, even though few questioned her level of competence. Clinton began the Democratic Party primary and caucus season as the presumed party favorite. She held a resounding lead in the polls over her rivals for the nomination in the beginning. In the final analyses, some cited her husband, former president Bill Clinton, and the distasteful scandals of his years in the White House as a huge campaign liability for her.

Barack Obama's campaign strategists must be given their due credit. They essentially out campaigned the Clinton machine. They used Obama's great attributes, such as his charisma, his articulation, and his ability to relate to voters to draw in huge numbers of new voters and supporters. They raised money at history-making levels and they infused the campaign with young, energetic, and activist voters. They used the Internet to effectively campaign in ways that the Internet had never been utilized for campaigning and fundraising purposes like never before. Obama's campaign generated thousands of new volunteers who served as an extremely effective door to door and traveling campaign army. An example of this was during the all-important Iowa caucus. The Iowa caucus was flooded with volunteers at each door. The Obama campaign was able to amass a huge national database of supporters and potential supporters, and they ran a superb text-messaging campaign. Volunteers could dispatch messages immediately. This proved to be a huge advantage for Team Obama during the 2008 Democratic presidential nomination race.

Feminists for Peace and Obama was one of several feminist organizations that decided to endorse Senator Obama's candidacy. The Democratic National Committee (DNC) was reportedly concerned that Black voters would protest and stay home if Senator Clinton got the nomination, even though she was seemingly the stronger and more electable candidate. But the DNC didn't seem to worry that White women, three times larger than the combined Black vote, would stay away from the polls if Mrs. Clinton did not get the nomination. They expected the White women of the party to fall in line and vote for Senator Obama in the general election.

Senator Hillary Clinton finished as the most successful female presidential candidate in U.S. history, garnering nearly 18 million votes in the process. No other female candidate has ever garnered as much support as she did while running for the presidential nomination of a major political party. Sarah Palin would go on to become the woman to receive the highest number of votes for any elective office in our history, garnering approximately 60 million votes as John McCain's running mate with the Republican Party. Senator Barack Obama said that Hillary Clinton inspired millions of Americans and was a shining example for his two young daughters, alluding to her history-making feat.

On June 3, 2008, Senator Barack Obama sealed the Democratic presidential nomination, coming one step closer to becoming the nation's first African American president. It was the culmination of a nearly two-year process of showing the American people that an African American man can indeed be a viable and victorious candidate for the office of president of the United States of America. Obama didn't just win the Democratic nomination; he transformed the American political landscape. His campaign demonstrated how social networking and technology could help to create a political whirlwind that could overwhelm even an established political dynasty.

The 2008 presidential campaign was one of the longest and most divisive ever. The result was a resurfacing of deep-rooted tensions and uneasiness regarding some historically challenging issues, which at many times revolved around race and gender. The hard fought battle opened the door for lingering questions to be answered involving the precise role of dual identities in American presidential politics. What role did race and gender play in the 2008 presidential election? The true role of race and gender, if any, may never be determined with absolute certainty. Undoubtedly, with two major candidates representing each identity in the race, the impact was obviously there. Many still believe staunchly that the 2008 presidential race was actually more about the core political issues of the day and a fatigued nation eager for some kind of change in their national leadership.

Chapter 10

An Influential New Voting Bloc Emerges

Power can be taken, but not given. The process of taking is empowerment in itself.

—Gloria Steinem

In the 2008 Pennsylvania Democratic primary, only 11 percent of African American women voted for Senator Hillary Clinton, compared to 64 percent of White women.[1] At the beginning of the 2008 Democratic primary season, African Americans felt a familiarity at the time with former president Bill Clinton and his administration, and they felt that Hillary Clinton of all of the candidates for president had the best chance of winning against the Republicans. Those feelings changed and a significant African American voter surge helped Senator Barack Obama to eventually win the Democratic nomination for president of the United States.

On August 29, 2008, Republican presidential nominee Senator John McCain announced his selection of Alaska governor Sarah Palin as his running mate. Palin, new to the national political scene, was a surprise pick, going by the standards of most seasoned political observers. Palin was the object of intense media scrutiny. Some Republicans had hoped that women who were dismayed by the fact that Hillary Clinton did not receive the Democratic nomination or that she did not get the vice presidential nod from Obama, would support the candidacy of another female major party candidate. They wanted her to be a Republican version of Hillary Clinton. Palin helped to balance the Republican ticket in terms of gender, age, and experience. Numerous women's groups came out hard against Palin's candidacy, citing her social conservatism as one of numerous concerns. Palin represented the conservative base of her party

and her blue-collar background touted a strong antiestablishment message. Palin's pro-life stance made supporting her candidacy problematic
for many women. The protection of reproductive rights for women is
a huge issue for the female electorate. Once the election results were in,
it became clear that the selection of Palin as McCain's running mate did
not shift White women to McCain, and that women in minority groups
favored Obama.

Sarah Palin's candidacy never really resonated with many African
American women. Some were taken aback by her self-imposed title of
hockey mom. Some suggested that the title was noninclusive of minority
and lower-income mothers. Palin's social conservatism was not in keep-
ing with the majority of the Black female electorate. Palin was a supporter
of teaching evolution and creationism in schools, capital punishment, and
the banning of abortion in almost all cases. Palin's views were in conflict
with the views of many women—women of color included. Palin's lack
of national exposure left many voters uneasy at the possibility of her serving as vice president under John McCain, who if he had won, would have
been the oldest president in history to enter office. Many others were taken
aback by her stump speeches attacking Obama through the vice presidential nominee's traditional role in attacking the opposition.

McCain had his own issues with the African American electorate. Running against the first serious African American contender for the presidency was an impossible task for McCain in terms of courting Black
voters. Then there was McCain's vote against the Martin Luther King Jr.
federal holiday and his vote to end a federal program that provided breast
cancer screenings, with breast cancer being a disease that more Black
women die from than any other group of women.

The Choice

Given the historic and unprecedented nature of the opportunity to elect
the first African American or the first woman as the Democratic nominee
for president, voters were intensely engaged in this presidential primary.
Women played a huge role in the party nomination process by accounting for at least 57 percent of the vote in every primary and caucus in the
Democratic Party in 2008.[2]

As late as December 2007, Hillary Clinton was much more popular than
Barack Obama among African American women, according to a series of
polls that were conducted by CBS television.[3] Hillary Clinton's base had

consistently been voters with lower income and less education and Barack Obama's base consisted mainly of voters with higher income and more education along with strong support eventually from African American voters. Many voters seemed drawn to his powerful call for change. They viewed him as something new and refreshing that is desperately needed in the new political landscape, particularly in contrast to a candidate such as Hillary Clinton.

African American women became the deciding factor in the South Carolina Democratic primary. Once Obama was able to win the Iowa caucus and African Americans began to see that White Americans would vote for an African American for president and that they began to envision the possibility that Obama could very well be elected president of the United States, they seemed to have been more willing to vote for him. Magazine covers such as that of *Ebony*, a leading Chicago-based publication whose targeted audience is African Americans, showed Obama's photo with the headline "In Our Lifetime." There began to be a monumental shift of support toward Senator Obama, particularly from African American voters. About 3 in 10 voters in the South Carolina primary were African American women.

There has also been speculation by many African Americans that the Clintons may have played the race card during the 2008 presidential campaign. Bill Clinton was quoted as saying, "Jesse Jackson won South Carolina too."[4] Many African Americans interpreted that as Bill Clinton trivializing Obama's significant primary victory in that state. They were outraged at what seemed like the former president's dismissal of Obama's candidacy. In actuality, Clinton was making more of the point that candidates that have won the South Carolina Democratic primary did not necessarily end up winning the nomination. Political pundits added a lot of spin to the statements and, coincidentally or not, millions of African Americans switched over to the Obama camp. Incidentally, near the end of the primary season, Clinton accused the Obama camp of playing the race card on him and accused them of planning to play the race card all along because the Obama camp used the statement to mobilize South Carolina's Black voters. African Americans had been a fiercely loyal constituency for President Clinton and the backlash that the Clintons received was unpredictable at the beginning of the presidential campaign.

There is a huge longing among African Americans to advance politically, as evidenced by the margin of the support for Barack Obama by African Americans in the 2008 presidential election. African American support for Barack Obama lingered around 95 percent during the election cycle.[5] Talk-show host Oprah Winfrey helped to sway many African American voters through her fervent support of Barack Obama. This strong showing of support of Obama by African Americans has caused some critics to conclude that race trumps gender most of the time for many women of color when it comes to major issues of the day.

Even as late as April 2007, some polls conducted during that time showed that more African American women were supporting Hillary Clinton among African American registered Democratic voters. The polls also showed that the largest amount of support for Clinton from African Americans derived from the support of African American women. Donna Brazile, Democratic strategist and former National Campaign Manager for former presidential candidate Al Gore, was quoted as saying, "The sistah vote is paying off handsomely for Hillary Clinton. It's not only getting her the women's vote. It's also getting her the black vote."[6] It did seem to some that once Clinton lost the African American female vote that the numbers of her overall female support base decreased somewhat significantly. Perhaps she could have won the nomination without the majority of the Black vote if she had had a higher percentage of the White vote, as some analysts suggest.

Historically, Black women have helped to decide the winners in state primaries where Black voters make up the majority of likely Democratic voters. This trend has been seen in various elections in states such as South Carolina, Georgia, Mississippi, and Alabama. For the first time, the impact of the African American female voting bloc had the distinction of having a heavy, direct, and course-changing impact on the outcomes of a national election cycle.

Many have found the premise insulting that Black women would make their decision as to who they vote for based upon their race or gender. Many claim that there is a balance in their decision-making—they take into account their desire to politically advance African Americans or women with the views and issues that each candidate represents. A report compiled by Spellman College indicated that less than 10 percent of African American, Latina, and other women of color responded that race or gender would be a primary motivator of selecting the next president of the United States.[7] The results from the survey, however, despite such a small percentage claiming these two factors would be primary motivators, would also allow one to conclude that African American women were more likely to support Obama, and Latina and other minority women were more likely to support Clinton as respondents indicated that race and gender would be primary factors in their choice of candidates to vote for in an election.

Wealthier and more educated women were more likely to move toward supporting Barack Obama, while working class and older women were more likely to vote for Hillary Clinton. Although many women did feel that Clinton was their best opportunity for seeing a woman in the Oval Office in their lifetime and that it would be a long time before another woman would be in a position to be seen as a viable candidate for the presidency of the United States, that did not necessarily sway their votes from Obama to Clinton. Clinton is viewed as solid and strong, some of the characteristics that women idealize for a female commander-in-chief. These very same traits are also seen as polarizing and threatening, as was remarked during Clinton's campaign for the presidency.

Skepticism of an Emerging African American Female Voting Bloc

A voting bloc in electoral politics is defined as a particular group of voters that vote collectively and cohesively to effect electoral outcomes. Voting blocs can hold candidates and officeholders accountable on policy issues by using their votes as political leverage. Views on current policies and issues oftentimes determine how a particular voting bloc may vote within an election cycle. Voting blocs can have an influential effect on election outcomes. As the size and support of a voting bloc grows so does its political strength and ability to influence election outcomes and government policy, in local, state, and national electoral contests.

Historically, the African American electorate functions as an active voting bloc in national elections where the vote is pretty evenly split among White voters. African American women have been identified as a key voting bloc within the Democratic Party. Black women are not characteristically single issue voters, but they are proven loyal supporters of the Democratic Party. For example, during the 2000 presidential race, in Illinois, George W. Bush won the White vote with 50 percent of the votes to Al Gore's 48 percent. Seven percent of the citizens who voted were African American; five percent of this number was African American women.[8] Ninety percent of African American voters voted for Al Gore, increasing his vote percentage to 51 percent over Bush.[9] A similar trend was consistent in several other states during the 2000 presidential election and when this trend occurred the winner was the Democratic Party candidate, Al Gore.

The 2004 Elections

As of 2004, 69 percent of eligible African Americans were registered to vote.[10] African Americans made up 11 percent of the total number of voters in the presidential election, but they made up 13 percent of all nonvoters.[11]

Black voters had been making some gains socioeconomically since the 1960s. In 2004, as compared to Whites, a lower percentage of Blacks had earned at least a high-school diploma (81% and 74% , respectively). More Black women than Black men had earned at least a bachelor's degree (16% compared with 13%), while among non-Hispanic Whites, a higher proportion of men than women had earned at least a bachelor's degree (26% and 23%, respectively).[12] Black voters delivered a significant increase in turnout during the 2004 elections from the previous elections in 2000. Black voters represented 12 percent of the total votes cast during the election in 2004.[13] This translated to approximately 14.6 million votes. Black women made up 52 percent of the total Black vote compared to 42 percent for Black men, demonstrating their influence within the African American electorate.[14] Studies indicated that Black women were the most loyal demographic within the Democratic Party base in several previous presidential elections.[15] Votes from Black women helped presidential candidate Al Gore to win several key states during the 2000 presidential election such as New York and Pennsylvania.[16] Also cited is Illinois where according to political analyst Yvonne Scruggs Leftwich, 10 percent of voters who were Black women helped Gore to win the state by 54 percent.[17]

Other Emerging Voting Blocs by Race

There is another voting bloc that is identified through both race and gender. Some political analysts suggest that Asian Americans may have emerged as an example of a crucial voting bloc during the 2008 California Democratic primary by helping Hillary Clinton to win the primary in that state. According to a CNN exit poll, about 75 percent of Asian voters cast their ballots for Clinton compared to 23 percent for Obama.[18] With Asians throwing their support behind her, Clinton carried 54 percent of the Democratic electorate in California, leading Obama by 14 percent in the state and significantly increasing her delegate count.[19] It has been noted that Asian women were particularly engaged in electing a female president. Yet the trend of voting for candidates for elective office that are the same racial make up that the voter is a trend that is more prominent among African Americans than any other major race group in this nation. The prevailing thought is that most African Americans voters vote along racial lines.

As far back as Reconstruction, the potential of the emergence of a potential voting bloc of African American women was abhorred. Mississippi senator J. K. Vardaman remarked, "The Negro woman will be more offensive, more difficult to handle at the polls, than the Negro man."[20] Because African American women do not define themselves as belonging exclusively to one political ideology, it is apparent that the candidates that they choose are heavily based on the issues of concern at hand. The best opportunities for new candidates to win an elective office are to compete for an open seat where the incumbent is not running for re-election or they are running in a newly created district.[21] Since most incumbents are White males, this trend blocks the arrival of many female and minority candidates for elective offices. The creation of a number of Black majority districts in 1991 was a major factor that opened the way for new Black representation on the Capitol Hill. New voting districts would favor the election of minority candidates from those districts and new Black officeholders emerged from those districts. It has been in these districts and others where the emerging African American female voting bloc has manifested itself to bring about change to the face of American politics.

Election dynamics are constantly changing. The Democratic primaries and caucuses of the 2008 presidential campaign were historic, drawing record turnouts, which resulted in more than 35 million voters participating in the process to select a Democratic presidential nominee. In the final analysis, we are still left to ponder the question, is that glass ceiling in politics tougher to break for females than it is for minorities who are male? The answer to the question may lie more in what the individual candidate brings to the election table as opposed to what their racial or gender make-up may be.

Chapter 11

A Renewed Sense of Obligation

The purpose of politics is to give people tools to make the most of their lives.

—Bill Clinton

The next time a woman runs, or a black, or a Jew or anyone from a group that the country is "not ready" to elect to its highest office, I believe that he or she will be taken seriously from the start . . . I ran because somebody had to do it first. In this country, everybody is supposed to be able to run for President, but that has never really been true.

—Shirley Chisholm

Senator Barack Obama sealed the Democratic presidential nomination on June 3, 2008. Just months before that historic date, the reality of an African American man becoming president of the United States was at most improbable. His historic feat has inspired and re-energized Americans of all lineages and backgrounds. African American women have been particularly energized, having the opportunity to vote for a woman and an African American during the 2008 primary season.

The race for the presidency in 2008 brought deep-rooted racial and gender divisions within the Democrat Party and the country to the surface. The polarization of entities within the country was discovered through the passions and fervor generated by this hard-fought nomination battle. The nation had already been energized and polarized by divisive issues such as the Iraq War, terrorism, global outsourcing, energy independence, taxes, and health care; and then both gender and race became factors.

The 2008 presidential election had the highest number of African American female voters than any other presidential election. *USA Today* exit polling showed that 96 percent of African American women voted for Barack Obama, compared to 69 percent of working women. This demographic played a critical role in delivering victories to Barack Obama in several key battleground states. A shift of fewer than 398,615 votes in seven states (Ohio, Florida, Virginia, Indiana, North Carolina, Colorado, and New Hampshire) would have given Senator John McCain a majority of 273 electoral votes.[1] CNN estimated that in the state of North Carolina, 100 percent of African American women voted for Obama, 13 percentage points higher than African American men.[2] In the swing state of Virginia, 94 percent of African American women voted for Obama, 5 percentage points higher than African American men. Likewise in Pennsylvania, African American women and men were equal in the percentages of their vote for Obama, but African American women made up a higher percentage of the electorate. The high voter turnout of African American women trickled down to state elections as well. For instance, 96 percent of African American women supported candidate Kay Hagan in North Carolina as compared to all women (55%) who supported Hagan.[3] Likewise in the North Carolina governor's race, 96 percent of African American women voted for Beverly Perdue, compared to 52 percent of other women. African American women made up 12 percent of the total electorate in the state of North Carolina.

In the U.S. Senate, there was a net gain of one seat for women, making the Senate 83 percent male. There were no net gains for women in state governorships. In the House of Representatives, there was a net gain of two seats for women. There were no gains in African American representation. African American and Asian representation remained virtually the same in the U.S. House of Representatives and in governorships although New Hampshire's state Senate now enjoys a female majority as a result of the recent elections. In North Carolina, women won seven statewide offices.

In the future, we will be able to determine if African American women who attain elective office will pursue a legislative agenda that is significantly different from their male colleagues of the same racial group. By examining the legislative actions of the African American Congresswomen who were elected in 1992 during the Year of the Woman, research shows that their priorities reflected a special sensitivity toward the poor.[4] During this time, about one-third of the African American community was living below the established poverty line. Among these Congresswomen's attempts to fight unemployment and crime was the economic stimulus package of March 1993, which provided $16.2 billion for public works projects, creating 150,000 new jobs in public housing, and canal road and railway construction, as well as a summer jobs program for teenagers and a scholarship program for poor students.[5]

Poverty is still a major issue for African Americans. It is particularly problematic for African American women since many of them are single mothers and heads of households. Families led by single parents typically have the highest poverty rates. According to the U.S. Census Bureau in 2005, the average household income for Whites was $50,622 compared to $30,939 for African Americans.[6] In fact, elderly women of all races are nearly twice as likely to be poor as are elderly men, and the risk of poverty increases as women age. Poverty rates are three times higher among older African American women (42%) as among older White women (14%). African American economic progress is impeded by teenage pregnancy, high incarceration, and homicide rates, which help to increase the numbers of one-parent households. African American women earn 15 percent less than White women and 10 percent less than African American men. Income is a key factor in presidential voting behavior in women.[7] Many women are the heads of households where their income is oftentimes the primary income. As a result, income levels and other socioeconomic-related issues are of primary concern to millions of African American and female voters. These voters face varying levels of economic fragility, job security, and the need for government aid affects their voting behavior.[8] These women want politicians to promote programs and legislation that will help to foster themselves and their families economically. For so long, African American women have seen the privilege of voting as a means of economic and social enfranchisement, attained through the improvement of their communities. The candidates who espouse and represent the issues most important to this particular group of women will receive the lion share of the votes from these particular women.

African American women's political attitudes are often shaped by motherhood experiences, marriage as well as marital status, civic involvement, volunteering, workplace, and religious experiences. Throughout history, African American women have formed their own organizations that were geared toward social and racial equality. These women have begun social reform in their communities when the government fell short, and they created the means to educate their own.[9] The National Council of Negro Women (NCNW) was founded in 1935 to address both national and international concerns for Black women. The NCNW connects four million women worldwide. These organizations create a powerful voice for Black women.

These organizations that focus on Black female advocacy also work toward attaining gender equality and promoting issues that address social change. Some organizations document the unsung achievements of African American women while others mobilize women to connect various aspects of social, political, and economic life. These organizations work as a network to promote the causes and uniqueness of Black women. The NCNW advocates for inclusion of African American female nominees to the Supreme Court. They also advocate for health and education, highlighting a national initiative on obesity.

African American women as a demographic are often divided by the variables of age, social class, and sexual orientation. These variables help to determine the issues that each subgroup prioritizes when selecting candidates to vote for elective office. Younger voters tend to focus on environmental issues and concern for accessibility to higher education. Members of the Black lesbian community care about many of the same issues as other Black women and the care about marriage equality and discrimination based upon sexual orientation. We must become more aware of the political variables that affect the circumstances of these demographics. Women must educate themselves in regards to candidates and their positions on quality of life issues and other issues paramount to them. The ties that bind many African American women include the legacy of a prolonged and protracted struggle against racial and gender oppression. When combined collectively, these ties allow African American women to vote and react politically in one general direction, hence the creation of a voting bloc. David Bostitis of the Joint Center for Economic and Political Studies has acknowledged the unrecognized power of the African American female vote. "Black women make up 60 percent of the total Black vote. And they're the Democrats' most loyal voting bloc," he said.[10]

In more recent years, we witnessed some historic firsts such as in 2008 when David Patterson became the first African American governor to take office in New York, and Deval Patrick became the first African American governor of Massachusetts the year before. Condoleeza Rice became the first African American woman to serve as secretary of state, in 2005. Colin Powell became the first African American to be appointed secretary of state in 2001. African American voters are helping to make a difference in what American politics looks like. These historic elections and appointments culminated with the election of the first African American president in the United States in 2008.

Increasing the Number of Women Running for Elective Office

As a result of the 1965 Voting Rights Act, which prohibited discriminatory voter registration practices, Black voter registration in many Southern states doubled. The number of African Americans elected to office in the South increased from 72 in 1965 to 2,000 in 1996 and to nearly 5,000 in 1993.[11] Variables such as education, age, and socioeconomic status affect the political participation of women. Educational attainment has helped to influence the political attitudes of African American women as well as the amount of political participation of African American women. These avenues allow these women exposure to networking and increased opportunities to participate politically and civilly. Being that minority women can be at a disadvantage financially, this at times decreases their amount of political participation. The availability of these women also factors into how much time they can devote to participating politically.

Many women have enormous difficulties in raising the significant amounts of money required for women to run for elective office. Many minority women are single mothers, making it problematic for them in many instances to commit large amounts of time toward mounting campaigns for public office, a necessary component to being successful in that particular realm. Also socioeconomic pressures and disadvantages also can prevent women from this subgroup from volunteering in local politics, sometimes a necessary step to getting their feet in the door. Volunteer activities include knocking on doors, attending community meetings, making public appearances, and so on. Dealing with the "good ole boy" network can be a daunting task for many female political office seekers. Women must also sacrifice their privacy as evidenced by Sarah Palin's family situations becoming public fodder.

Organizations that recruit women for office are often few in number and these organizations are oftentimes underfunded for the enormous task of catapulting more minorities into elective office. There are those that argue that in seeking and recruiting diversity in presenting candidates for office when all is said and done, we ensure that is how we will produce the best qualified candidates for elective office. In the final analysis, women are underrepresented in the elective office positions because they simply don't run for office in high enough numbers.

Reflections

Victoria Woodhull and Belva Lockwood sought the office of president of the United States in the late 19th century. They were trailblazers for women seeking elective office during a time when women were not even allowed to vote. The public discourse at that time in our history was vehemently against females running for office. They faced both public ridicule and failure. However, they saw their candidacies as a vehicle for garnering public support for particular reforms rather than as a chance to win public office.[12] Following the women's suffrage movement, more women saw the feasibility of holding elective office.

The current boundaries of politics are being broken with each day that passes. It has only been in recent decades where African American women have received consistent voting access. Increased voter participation is something that African American women will use as a viable vehicle for change for decades to come. African American women are confident in their abilities as a group. There is a renewed sense of obligation on behalf of African American women to continue the progress and the gains that we have made since the Emancipation Proclamation and the passage of the Nineteenth Amendment. History says that the progress of race or gender will not proceed without the involvement of African American women.

Chapter 12

The Fulfillment of the Thirteenth and Nineteenth Amendments

Children today will grow up taking for granted that an African American or a woman can yes, become President of the United States.

—Hillary Clinton

On a National Organization for African American Women (NOAW) survey, women were asked what the impact was of having two very prominent women running for president and vice president in 2008:

It was powerful and enlightening. They were both extremely intelligent. The elections happened during a time when I began appreciating more about politics because some of the initiatives hit close to home so I felt as though I was a part of women on the move for change.

I believe that African American women were not valued, there was no major outreach to us. I was not impressed at all. I am glad an African American male was elected rather than a White woman.

It reminded people of the inequality that still exists in gender politics.

Contrary to popular belief, I didn't feel that there were two prominent women taking part of the 2008 election. Hillary Clinton is and always will be a phenomenal woman. Sarah Palin was comical and the act hasn't stopped. The election was an endeavor for Mrs. Clinton, but as to the impact for African American women, the mass majority of African Americans' attention was focused on the presidential hopeful, Mr. Barack Obama.

It was a step in the right direction. We need women to stand up and be that voice for others to follow.

It would seem to indicate that "change" is here; Is that true?

While I was thrilled to have the choice of very qualified women running. I still believed that Barack Obama was the best choice because of his platform for inclusion.

Honestly, I didn't feel really connected to Hillary, but more so to Cynthia McKinney. The media downplayed after running for President, but I was strengthened knowing she took that step.

None because the VP pick was in my opinion a sham. Give us a choice between two women of substance and that makes an impact. Not someone who is marginally qualified and can only use the lowest common denominator to win votes.

It gave women a better sense of seeing themselves having power in this country.

Hillary Clinton's campaign was positive for women in general. Sarah Palin's campaign's was not.

As an African American woman I didn't feel that having two prominent women in this presidential election this year brought such an impact on Black women.

It appears to me that we were more divided on the issues than understanding the concept of a woman running for office.

The impact of Hillary Clinton was substantial for women in general. I do feel that it got outweighed by Barack's run. As far as Palin, she was selected for the wrong reasons and her run was a reflection of that. She was horrible and embarrassing.

I honestly think it created a bit of a dilemma . . . i.e. who to vote for stick with gender or vote from a perspective of color! It was not an issue for me but I saw the battle amongst other females.

New doors were opened for women and Blacks but I think that we are a long way off from having a Black female President. Not sure this country is ready for it based on some of the "difficulty" America seemed to have with embracing Michelle Obama.

It provides hope for little girls, but I wasn't a fan of either and am glad that the right person won!

There was little to no impact for African American women in having two Caucasian women run for President and Vice President.

It was an amazing accomplishment but neither represented the plight of Black women very well.

There was only one prominent woman running for office. And I still think even though she's a woman, she doesn't represent the Black woman.

I believe that Michelle Obama as First Lady has had more of an impact on African American women than Clinton and Palin running. Shirley Chisholm also ran for President which for me would be more significant. Though I do not discount the historical context.

I did not lean towards either candidate. I was really not interested in voting for either of them.

Major impact for myself when I think about the lives of my children, grandchildren, etc.

For me it was not about gender but who would best be able to lead our country in the event they were in the seat.

It was a milestone for not only Black women, but all women!

For women there was a great impact, but African American women did not gain a big stand due to the two women running.

I feel that it held a great impact on women in general. For African American women I feel it gave an extra assurance that we can do it.

The impact for African American women of having Clinton and Palin involved with this year's election is that knowledge that women can aspire to high office and have the funds and people to support such a campaign.

On the contrary, I cannot fathom that there was any significant impact for women of color. Two women yes, neither one a woman of color. Only one had the potential to be President while the other embarrassed women by trying to get by on looks instead of intellect.

It had a great impact. For the younger and older generation because the younger can see that they can do anything their hearts desire. The older women because they've seen that they can also do anything, but can see that they have made an impact on the very changes and opportunities that are available for women today.

Neither woman spoke to issues that affect African American women. Clinton tried to appeal to the White working class by using divisive rhetoric. Palin spoke about "real Americans" a coded term that applied only to White Americans in the middle section of the country. The impact, if any, was to see the extent to which both parties are willing to throw African Americans under the bus to achieve their political goals.

I was a Hillary Clinton supporter initially, but her politics and tactics got way too dirty. As a woman, I expected her to show more cunning and grace. As far as Palin is concerned, I honestly saw her as an embarrassment to White women as a whole. I found nothing relatable about her whatsoever.

It was good to see that times have changed where women are becoming more prominent, especially in politics. I don't know what impact it was for African American women but for me, it made me feel like I may have a chance if I was to go in that direction.

Profound, it left a feeling of completeness and being a part of the whole process.

It allowed women to have a chance to be in the forefront of the political arena and it helped break the barriers of a male-dominated world.

It was good to see that we have come so far as a nation. These events are coming more commonplace as time goes on.

It was a phenomenal impact for ALL women of color. It reignited our souls and reminded each of us that we have not only a purpose and plan for our lives but more importantly that we have the power within to support and live out our purpose.

Realize that you cannot be equal—you must be better than your male competition to advance. Advancement in a male dominated world frequently is based upon principles most men learn as they grow up. Black women who fail to understand the importance of office politics, going through the proper channels, and being able to make decisions quickly put themselves at an automatic disadvantage. Life is a game which is not always fair for women but because of this election the good old boys environment will eventually find themselves at a competitive disadvantage with rivals who promote more competent, underpaid Black females to do the same kind of work. While opportunities for women have improved considerably, it remains clear that the doors to the top are not always open to them.

None. You saw for yourself that Americans would vote for a Black man, rather than voting for a woman. I didn't particularly care for either female candidate.

Women, especially women of color, are moving closer to the reality of being elected to higher political office in this country.

Women in the race for President and Vice President were very influential to African American women because it gave a sense of history moving forward and being more accepting of the female gender.

The impact was wonderful. It shows that we can get out there and do the JOB.

I was not impressed. I was rather offended, as a woman by Palin whom I felt did not speak for me. As excited as I was for Clinton, I believe she played the sexism card when convenient and I didn't support the "pantsuit club." I felt as if she sacrificed her femininity and fed into the good ole boys concept.

I was inspired because I was able to witness history. Knowing that women are finally being taken seriously. They are actually being judged by the content of their character and not by their sex.

While I consider it a milestone and am certainly appreciative of the doors that were opened for this to occur, I must say that some damage was done because the two were not the RIGHT ones to make our case.

Sarah Palin came off as incompetent—which most rebels against women in political office have claimed for decades/centuries.

I was very proud and inspired to review my career goals and ambitions.

It was very comforting knowing that change was in progress.

I think Hillary Clinton's run was important for all women regardless of skin color. I also think it showed that sexism does exist and that some of it can come from the Democratic Party, progressives, and the liberal media.

Personally, I don't think there was an impact or that I felt overwhelming sense of womanhood, as for America, women of different races have their own struggles.

It was inspiring and motivational.

Only superficially empowering. As ultimately it is not so much about gender or race, but about which economic class one is in when it comes to gaining power in the USA.

Well, as being Black women we already have two strikes against us. Not only are we Black, we are also women. I just think that the fact that women are being represented in a different light gives me a ray of hope. Seeing women do great things is an aspiration. Whether they are Republican or Democrat.

I felt that it was a very proud and significant moment because of both the historical implications. Women have been seen as incompetent and unqualified and as if we don't measure up to men. However, the women in the race portrayed our growth as a nation and our belief in the abilities of women.

I personally don't think that the two candidates in this election were going to have much of an impact for African-American women.

I think that the significance of the two women that ran and its impact on African American women is that our time is coming also. All we have to do is look back a little bit at Shirley Chisholm and fast forward to today to see that progress is imminent and that's awesome.

The 2008 presidential election has given new light to the unique posture of African American women. Eventually, there were to be two primary candidates in the Democratic race for the presidency, in which African American women could visualize in either candidate a distinct part of themselves. For the first time ever in American presidential politics, there was a definitive choice between their dual identities of race and gender.

The electorate in the 2008 elections in the United States was the most diverse in history. African Americans increased their representation in the electorate. They represented 12.1 percent of the electorate in 2008 compared to 11 percent in 2004. Of all voters, 76.3 percent in 2008 were White compared to 79.2 percent in 2004. This was the lowest share of the electorate that was White in the nation's history.[1]

The African American voter turnout rate was five points higher in 2008 compared to 2004 from 65.2 percent to 60.3 percent. For the first time in history, African American female voters participated in the election at the highest rate among all voters. The turnout rate among eligible African American female voters rose from 63.9 percent in 2004 to 68.8 percent in 2008. This diversity was caused in large part by population growth among numerous ethnic groups between the years of 2004 and 2008. Of the African American voters, 24.3 million were eligible to vote in 2008 compared to 22.9 million in 2004.[2]

In the 1950s, only 37 percent of Americans said they would vote for a Black for president.[3] American society has made tremendous strides in terms of racial and gender discrimination in the decades since the 1950s. Senator Barack Obama had to overcome the skepticism of many African Americans that a man of color could not only embark on a viable campaign for a major party's nomination but that a man of color could be elected president of the United States. We now live in a time where members of specific racial and gender groups that could only dream of having serious presidential aspirations are now having millions of voters cast their votes for them in a presidential primary.

The African American woman has played a tremendous part in the foundations of African American history, life, and culture. She has stood loyally and defended her men, her family, her church, her communities, her gender, and lastly, herself. She has survived the brutality of the Middle Passage, withstood the inhumanity of slavery, tasted the immeasurable joy of freedom, struggled to uplift her family through the Depression, fought for equal and civil rights, and somehow, miraculously, survived it all.

Shirley Franklin became the first African American woman in U.S. history to be elected mayor of a large city in a Southern state in large part due to the large amount of support that she received from Black women. In 2001, African American women galvanized behind Franklin to catapult her into the mayor's office. African American women are the largest demographic of voters in the city of Atlanta making up almost 30 percent of registered voters in the city.[4] It can be argued that Black women's support for Franklin was key in her electoral victory in the mayoral race. The voting bloc of African American women played a key role in her historic election.

Despite the passages of the Fourteenth and Fifteenth Amendments, which established voting rights for African Americans, for decades, many African Americans particularly in the South, were disenfranchised due to established roadblocks to voting, the most popular methods being the poll tax and literacy tests. A major goal of the civil rights movement was the Voting Rights Act. On August 6, 1965, President Lyndon Johnson signed the Voting Rights Act into law. Within one month of the Act's passage, almost 30,000 African Americans registered to vote. African American candidates for elective office were the primary beneficiaries of the passing of the Voting Rights Act. African Americans elected Black Congressmen, mayors, and state officials in unprecedented numbers.

Until 1993, there were never more than four Black women serving in Congress at the same time.[5] Between the 1993 and the 1998 elections, there were 12 African American women in the U.S. House of Representatives and one, Carol Moseley Braun, in the U.S. Senate. Carol Moseley Braun was elected in 1992, the infamous Year of the Woman where a record number of women were elected to Congress.[6]

Candidates who seek the plurality of the votes of the African American electorate, regardless of their race or gender, must foster stronger connections with the African American community. Candidates who come across as being capable and reliable and who focus on issues such as health care, jobs, and education will resonate much stronger with the African American community. The African American must be energized for candidates to successfully receive the votes of the African American electorate.

African American women are trailblazers not just in politics, but also in various fields and many different walks of life. Madame C. J. Walker, the first Black female millionaire and legendary Black businesswoman was by the standard of many, the most successful Black entrepreneur of her time. Walker was a trailblazer to another iconic African American woman, Oprah Winfrey, has achieved the unthinkable. She is the most powerful woman in the entertainment industry and she is a member of this distinct dual identity group. Winfrey is just one shining example of how far we have come as a race and as women.

Americans were inspired and proud of how our nation has progressed to have had both a woman and a man of color as serious contenders for the nomination for president for the Democratic Party in 2008. With this milestone comes a renewed sense of obligation for African American women to expand on the achievements of such an historic election. African American women have had major roles in the progression of both race relations and feminism. Their contributions have been largely understated by history. The extraordinary journey of African American women in the face of racial and gender oppression is a testimony to the resilience of determined women. Educational opportunities and economic progress have allowed African American women to progress tremendously and allowed many Black women to excel and contribute to the greater good of this nation. Women have a rich and extensive history of political activism in social movements and civic organizations in the United States. The true impact of the sacrifice and fortitude of African American women in the most profound social movements of the last two centuries has been immeasurable.

African American Voter Influence

The 10 states with the largest Black population in 2006 were New York, Florida, Texas, Georgia, California, Illinois, North Carolina, Maryland, Virginia, and Michigan.[7] Combined, these 10 states represented 49 percent of the total Black population.[8] Of the 10 largest places in the United States with a population of 100,000 or more, Detroit had the largest proportion of Blacks (83%) followed by Philadelphia (44%) and Chicago (38%).[9] These are states where the African American electorate has and can have tremendous impact on election outcomes. Due to the success in increasing African American voter registration following the passage of the Voting Rights Act, registering voters has become a vital strategy for getting more African American candidates into elective office. The trends of the last few decades indicate that it is quite beneficial to African Americans in particular, to elect candidates for office who will directly address the issues and matters of critical importance to the African American electorate. Voting is powerful. This transcends into the ability to enact laws and create programs that will uplift African Americans economically, socially, and politically. If you don't vote, you most likely will not be heard. Voting gives voice to the downtrodden and the disenfranchised. Voting is true individual power in this nation. The African American electorate, particularly African American women, have yet to fully utilize its full potential for impact within American electoral politics because most African American are probably not fully aware of its position. If more African American women become more aware of their voting power and influence, more of these women would mobilize to effect change within the political mainstream.

African Americans are in a unique position socially and politically. Institutional racism, race-based prejudices, discrimination, and the dehumanization of African Americans through the institution of slavery have made the journey of African American men and women problematic. The trauma and indignities of racial oppression has made African American women seem instinctively to work toward the progression of their race by oftentimes being slightly indifferent to their respective gender issues. It should be clear today as to how the distinct social, political, economic, and cultural experiences influence their political outlook.[10] History helps to dictate the course of African American women in politics.

The question remains: Does racial discrimination and gender subordination play a role in the lower numbers of African American women in elected office? Perhaps, but African American women must continue the fight to get more Black women into elective office regardless of assumptions. The sense of obligation that African Americans feel toward electing the first African American is potent and heartfelt. A similar obligation is felt toward electing the first woman to the presidency in our lifetime. One can attempt to balance the weight of that obligation by allowing the analysis of the issues and the candidates' values to guide their decision of which candidate will be their best choice for president. Issues that are important to women voters were prominent in the 2008 presidential campaign. Education, equal pay, health care, and economic well-being were first and foremost in the minds of American female voters.

Do traditional party mechanisms work to enhance the prospects for African American woman in attaining elective office? Political parties must commit themselves to recruiting more women and minority women to run for elective office. Practices of political parties and how candidates are selected greatly impacted the candidacies of women for elective office. Many theorize that women with families find it more problematic to pursue elective office. More women of color should begin by running for local office, since it is most likely an easier road to get elected into office, and that incumbents stand a far better chance than untested challengers in an electoral race.

Numerous conditions make the pursuit of elective office problematic for many women, particularly for women of color. Few minorities hold critical positions within party organizations. Putting together, the money and the organization is a huge obstacle to many female and minority candidates. Undoubtedly, we live in a patriarchal society as evidenced by the fact that a woman who is by all standards the first viable female candidate for president is seen as groundbreaking. Clinton's campaign slogan, "Help make history," is a direct reference to the historic relevance of her candidacy. Female candidates are more likely to act on behalf of women's issues and concerns. Women must become more aware of the political variables that affect their circumstances. They must commit to educate and re-educate themselves in regards to candidates for elective office and their positions of contemporary quality of life issues.

African American women are an identity group with two distinct and distinguishable identities. Each identity comes with its own specific core histories and issues. The argument remains that race trumps gender in terms of political philosophy, ideology, and activism. One day, undoubtedly, sooner than we would have thought just four years ago, a member of this dual identity group will herself be a viable candidate for president from a major political party.

Where Do African American Female Voters Stand?

Will African American women support a candidate who looks like them or with someone who feels their pain and identifies with and represents the issues that they are concerned about? Is it more difficult for African Americans to penetrate racial stereotypes and barriers, as opposed to women having to penetrate gender stereotypes and barriers? Take the Senate for instance. There have only been three African American U.S. senators compared to the dozen or so women U.S. senators. Currently, there are eight White females and one African American male serving as governors of states in the United States. And again, the eight females serving today greatly outnumber the two African American male governors elected since Reconstruction. White women are more likely to attain elective office in higher numbers than their dual identity counterparts.

Feminist organizations have been accused of ignoring the condition of women of color in general, making collaboration on shared interests sometimes problematic. Many believe that feminists do not comprehend the magnitude of the burden of race on women of color. Part of the frustration of many African American women was the lack of acknowledgment of racism on behalf of many feminist organizations. There have been common struggles for social and political empowerment through these movements. Black women, as history demonstrates, were secondary in both the women's suffrage movement and the civil rights movement. African American women have undoubtedly contributed to the overall empowerment of all women.

Sexism and racism have compounded the efforts of empowerment for African American women for many decades. The preponderance of their dual identity group status increases the odds that African American women will face some form of discrimination of some point in their lives, since they deal with both racial and gender issues. This unique and now powerful voting bloc can no longer be ignored as it has been in decades past. Many African American women are looking beyond the layers of race and gender. They want their voices to be heard and they want their issues to be addressed. Is there a political glass ceiling for African American women in politics? Is that ceiling different than the ceilings that African American men and White women have to penetrate to ascend to the highest office in the land?

The tridimensional issues of race, gender, and class have an impact on the progress of women politically. These distinctive paradigms overlap in a manner that hampers the progress within one without progress in another. Black feminism developed as a result of the combination of the racial, gender, sexual, and economic oppression of Black women. Class issues among African American women must be recognized and appropriately acknowledged so that the economic challenges of African American women can be adequately assessed. We must find ways to accommodate diversity among women, particularly in the area of race. Within the African American female electorate there are younger African American women, gays and lesbians, and seniors. Each subgroup at times has their own distinct priorities and concerns. African American women have a dual identity and these identities intersect. Being Black does not take away from the undeniable fact that African American women are also women. Their race *and* their gender have distinct histories, obstacles, characteristics, and needs. Their race and gender needs and obstacles intersect a lot, particularly politically. The interests of their race are oftentimes in conflict with the needs of their gender.

Are men convinced that women are incapable of successfully holding and maintaining positions of power? The political environment has been somewhat hostile to African American female candidates for elective office. A 2006 Gallop poll indicated that 61 percent of Americans say that they are ready to elect a woman president.[11] Few African American women attain political leadership through elective office.

Historically, it has been argued that African American women worked primarily for their race, while White women worked for their gender. Slavery, disenfranchisement, racial discrimination, and lynchings, among other hardships, kept the issues of racial oppression in the forefront for Black women. African American women have historically subordinated their interests as women for the sake of the African American community, as evidenced by the reluctance of Black women to force themselves to the forefront of social movements such as the civil rights movement. The civil rights movement perpetrated strict gender roles for women within the movement. African American men and women did not stand together as legitimate equals during the civil rights movement in the fight against racial oppression. In this movement and others for the fight for racial equality, Black women neglected many feminist ideals. In fact, many Black women frowned upon even identifying themselves as feminists. For many Black women, Black womanhood has its foundations in the Black family. Adopting feminist ideology was seen by many within the Black community as an assault on Black family and Black men. For these reasons, one can conclude that within as well as outside of the African American community that race has historically trumped gender in the political and social arenas, which is reflective of the struggles of African American women against oppression.

The debate is ongoing concerning the connections of race, class, and gender within major social and political systems in the United States. These ideological justifications espouse that gender, racism, and feminism merge in an obtuse manner. African American women must navigate the interlocking obstacles of race, gender, and class in context with their concrete historical experiences as members of specific race, class, and gender groups. There needs to be a reexamination of how racism, sexism, and classism simultaneously work to manifest the other. There is a growing demand to foster interracial cooperation among women of all social and economic backgrounds. African American women may not alter their voting preferences but their experiences do impact how likely they would be to relate to and identify with the candidates that they choose to support for elective office. Continued and increased political activism is necessary for African American women to empower themselves politically. Black women should be at the forefront of controlling the Black Women's agenda by shaping the strategy, tactics, roles, and values that they espouse as both African Americans and as women within their political parties.

There are in more instances than not a different set of life experiences for Black women than has been experienced by the traditional candidate for elective office. Although African American women are disproportionately affected by issues such as poverty, discrimination, and health concerns, the sharing of mutual issues of concern is beneficial to women of all ethnicities. The struggle for African American women must connect with the larger feminist movements to effect positive and measurable change and we must continue to fight to create an environment to address gender oppression without seeming to attack men in the process.

Adequate appropriation of resources and education are crucial for the continued political mobilization of African American women. Educated and informed voters are unlikely to vote for a candidate because they are female or because they are of a certain race. Senator Hillary Rodham Clinton garnered more votes in a presidential primary than any other previous female candidate in history. Many African American women played a role in the attainment of this historic feat by Senator Clinton. Women in America are not just White women; African American women and women of other ethnicities are undeniably part of the very large and influential demographic as well for they share an ideological kinship.

There are varying expressions of African American women's actions in countering the challenges of oppression. African American women have discovered a newfound voice in American politics. Having historically manifested political mobilization through social movements, civic organizations, and organized religious networks, African American women are now mobilizing politically through the ballot box. Voting rearticulates the interdependence of these women's experiences and their consciousness as a dual identity group and represents a partial perspective of the changing needs of this demographic. Black women voters have distinct issues, concerns, and voting interests that are at times separate from other voting blocs. The candidate who understands what it is like to be a Black woman in 21st century America will win the support of this empowered voting bloc.

Taking Full Advantage of the African American Female Vote

Ida B. Wells encouraged African American women to use their vote for the advantage of themselves and their race. African American women and men are a very large and loyal constituency within the Democratic Party. Historically, African Americans vote predominantly for candidates of the Democratic Party. Through the research of Jewel Prestige, it is known that African American women participate in the voting process at a higher rate than African American men.[12] The gap in voting and registration between African American men and women is slightly larger than the 2.5 percentage point difference in voting and registration evident between White men and women.[13] African American women have become conditioned to being ignored and sidelined in so many different facets of their everyday lives. As a major deciding factor in numerous national and state elections in 2008, African American women should now be propelled towards full inclusion in the American political mainstream.

The 2008 presidential election was unique in many ways. It was the first time since 1928 that an incumbent did not run for the presidential or vice presidential nomination of their party. It was the first time that an African American man's primary rival for the nomination of a major party was a woman. It was the first time that an African American man won the nomination of a major political party for president in the United States. It was the first time that a woman ran for vice president of the United States on the Republican Party presidential ticket. The 2008 Democratic presidential primaries and caucuses were electrifying. Emotions ran extremely high on all sides. If you disliked the Black candidate, people had a tendency to perhaps perceive you as racist. If you disliked the female candidate, then people had the tendency to perhaps see you as sexist. This historic election is a testament of what can happen when race and gender collide. There was overwhelming emotion in the African American community for the candidacy of Barack Obama. To many African Americans, Obama's election was the culmination of the continued struggle for racial equality and the fulfillment of the dream of overcoming racial inequality.

Eight million more women voted for Senator Obama than Senator McCain. Women, particularly young women, may think we have achieved some measure of equality but you only have to look around you to see who still holds the vast majority of economic, political, and social power— it isn't women and that may be why Clinton faced such a huge backlash because she dared to tread on male territory and threaten to take some of their power. Feminist icon Gloria Steinem summed up her reflections upon this unprecedented election cycle: "I mean, I really think that we have seen historically that women of color, African American women, have understood—have been just in a better position, you know, to understand the roles of both sex and race, and it made me nostalgic for the days of Shirley Chisholm and campaigning for Shirley Chisholm."[14]

Was the 2008 presidential election about the unprecedented challenge of choosing between two identities for Black women? Many believed the 2008 presidential election to have been as much about contemporary issues and political values as it was about the candidacies. Regardless of political perspective, African American women have had the honor of experiencing tremendous pride in the historic campaigns of an African American man and a woman running for the highest office in the land. A milestone in our nation's history has been reached. This presidential election has been a catalyst for a new conversation on the impact of race and gender on American politics. Was race and gender a major issue in this campaign? According to former San Francisco mayor Willie Brown, it was:

> Yes, race is an issue in this campaign. Race will be an issue in this campaign if Barack Obama is the nominee. If Hillary Clinton is the nominee, gender will be an issue in this campaign and you better recognize it and be clear, gender is less suspect to the body politic and less suspect to the body politic than race. But, it is still a five percent handicap. Race is probably a ten percent handicap.[15]

Was the 2008 presidential election a referendum on race and gender? The question remains not whether or not race and gender matter today in the world of American politics, but rather the question is *how* do they matter? These are viable and extenuating twin issues for African American women. African American women looked beyond the layers of race and gender and voted for the candidate that they believed thought that they and their issues *mattered.* Most African American women have a different set of life experiences from the traditional candidate for elective office and their political dynamic is dictated by these life experiences. African American women have been pushed into the background for generations in the name of the advancement of race, family, and community. For that reason, we must strive as a society for gender balance in American politics. The movement to ensure that all women are equal participants in American politics grows stronger with each election cycle. In time, the glass ceiling won't be cracked; it will be permeated all the way through.

On the November 4, 2009, gubernatorial election in the Commonwealth of Virginia, Black voter turnout decreased to 16 percent from 20 percent in the 2008 presidential election.[16] This was the lowest turnout for Black vote in a gubernatorial election in almost 40 years. A prominent African American female, Sheila Johnson, gave Republican gubernatorial candidate Bob McDonnell her endorsement. The Black vote, historically so critical to Democratic Party electoral success, was not energized. However, African Americans remain the most loyal Democratic Party voters.[17]

Chapter 13

The 2008 Presidential Election: The Choice

As an African American woman, I didn't feel that having two prominent women in this Presidential election this year brought such an impact on Black women. It appears to me that we were more divided on the issues than understanding the concept of a woman running for office.

—Anonymous

Many African American women felt that the 2008 presidential election was a powerful testament toward progress for both African Americans and the female gender. People felt that they were part of a broader movement for change. The increase in African American voter participation in 2008 was driven mostly by increased voter activity among African American women and younger voters. The Pew Research Center reports that overall, among all ethnic and gender groups, African American women had the highest voter turnout rate in the presidential election for the first time ever.[1]

Barack Obama engaged and infused young people into his campaign as never seen before in a presidential race. Many younger voters felt that their concerns were being heard and that their call for change was taken seriously. Numerous feminist leaders and organizations supported Barack Obama for president, over his female competitor for the Democratic nomination. Leading feminist groups such as National Association for the Repeal of Abortion Laws enthusiastically endorsed Obama instead of Hillary Clinton.

The election of 2008 remade the American political landscape. There was a major realignment in American politics. There was also an unprecedented choice for all Americans, including Black women in that historic presidential election cycle, as it related to both their race and their gender.

Never before had there been an African American male and a female who had both mounted serious campaigns for the presidential nomination within a major political party simultaneously.

The Choices for President and Vice President

Many African American women responded to polling that they did not feel the impact of having two prominent women taking part in the 2008 presidential election:

> Hillary Clinton is and always will be a phenomenal woman. Sarah Palin was comical and the act still hasn't stopped. The election was an endeavor for Mrs. Clinton, but as to the impact for African American women, the mass majority of African Americans attention was focused on the presidential hopeful, Barack Obama.[2]
>
> The Vice Presidential pick was in my opinion a sham. Give us a choice between two women of substance and that makes an impact. Not someone who is marginally qualified and can only use the lowest common denominator to win votes.[3]

Hillary Clinton ended up receiving millions of votes during the Democratic primaries and caucuses, garnering the most votes for any female candidate in American history in a major party nomination contest. Sarah Palin would surpass that by garnering millions more while on the Republican Party ballot for vice president of the United States. Hillary Clinton was heavily criticized for divisive rhetoric during the 2008 Democratic primaries and caucuses, including the renowned incident where her husband and former president Bill Clinton was criticized for declaring that Jesse Jackson also won the South Carolina primary, making the implication that if Obama won, it may prove to be just as insignificant. Sarah Palin used the term *real* Americans, which caused some to accuse her of divisiveness as well. In fact, much of Palin's campaign base was male-dominated. For Palin, being a woman was not nearly enough incentive in itself to have many African American women switch parties to vote for a female candidate for vice president. Some African American women responded that they felt that they were not valued. They complained of having no specific major outreach toward African American women from either major party female candidate. Black women in some instances were reminded of the level of inequality that continues to exist in modern politics.

Despite the fact that both Hillary Clinton and Sarah Palin did not win their respective offices, they did, however, have a permanent impact on the electoral landscape for the female candidates for elective office that come after them. Hillary Clinton garnered over 17 million votes in her bid for the Democratic nomination for president (breaking the previous record for a candidate seeking the Democratic nomination) and Sarah Palin earned approximately 60 million votes on the Republican Party ticket as the vice presidential candidate. Female office seekers are no longer deterred from how many of their campaigns may be termed symbolic. Women will continue to demonstrate that they can indeed be both viable and ultimately successful candidates for elective office, including major ones such as president or vice president.

Recent Efforts by Established Black Female Candidates

Cynthia McKinney

The media downplayed her running for President, but I was strengthened, knowing that she took that step.

—Anonymous

Cynthia McKinney was the Green Party candidate for president in the 2008 presidential election and she happens to be an African American female. McKinney first ran for a state congressional seat in Georgia in 1988. Her father was already a member of the state legislature, making them the only father-daughter state legislators during that time period. In 1992, McKinney became the first African American woman to represent Georgia in the U.S. House of Representatives when she was elected to Congress that year. McKinney went on to serve six terms in the U.S. House of Representatives.

McKinney is known for her trademark braided hairstyle. She is also known for her at times controversial stands against the Bush administration and her allegations of voter fraud during the more recent presidential elections. She was also a vocal opponent of the Iraq War. During the 2000 presidential campaign, McKinney wrote that "Gore's Negro tolerance level has never been too high. I've never known him to have more than one black person around him at any given time."[4] Gore was quick to point out at the time that his campaign manager at times was Donna Brazile who is an African American woman.

Rosa Clemente became her running mate, making them the first all-female of color ticket for a major political party ticket. Rosa Clemente is of African American and Puerto Rican descent. Cynthia McKinney received approximately 162,000 votes in the presidential election, making her the African American female who has garnered the most votes ever for president of the United States. McKinney was lost, so to speak, under the glare of the first African American male with a viable opportunity to ascend to the presidency along with the first female candidate. The presidential election of 2008 didn't just produce the history making candidacies of the most successful African American male and female candidates for president from a major political party, but also produced the most successful African American female candidate for president from a large political party.

Julia Williams

Newcomers to the electoral stratosphere are continuing to emerge. Julia Williams was a candidate for the Register of Wills in the September 14, 2010, primary in Prince Georges County, Maryland. Williams has been an educator for well over 15 years. She has also worked quite successfully as an exemplary mentor and tutor in the foster care system. She shared some of the experiences that she had as an African American female first-time candidate for local elective office. Williams provides an inside view of the difficulties of running for office as a novice to the electoral process.

Q: Julia, what made you decide initially to run for office?

A: A business partner of my husband's asked me to run for office. Initially, he had asked me to run for the School Board but after I realized that it would instantly be a scheduling conflict with my current job, I decided to run for the position of Register of Wills.

Q: What were your biggest obstacles during your candidacy?

A: I had a lack of money raised for the campaign and I decided to throw my hat into the ring very late in the campaign season. Most of the other candidates had been campaigning for at least a year or so. I also knew that it was going to be very tough to beat the incumbent because of their family and political connections.

Q: Did you feel like there were certain obstacles that were specific to you being a female candidate?

A: No, I do not feel there were particular obstacles that were gender-specific.

Q: What is your background?

A: I possess a master's degree in public administration and I have worked for over a decade as an educator in the public school system. I do not have a political background. However, I had a little political experience volunteering with Anthony Williams's campaign for mayor of the District of Columbia. I also volunteered for the presidential campaign for Barack Obama in Howard County, Maryland.

Q: Did any of your recent experiences catapult you into entering the primary?

A: I saw firsthand how politics control every aspect of our lives.

Q: Given your recent experiences being a candidate for office, why do you think more women do not run for elective office?

A: Running for office a lot of time and commitment. That is something that most women do not have especially if they are married with children or a single mother. Even if you are a single woman, it takes a way from your current job. That can sometimes cause problems or put your job in jeopardy if you are not successful in the race. This in turn can be a huge financial setback.

Q: Who are some of the women in politics that you admire, nationally or locally?

A: I admire Representative Maxine Waters, Fannie Lou Hamer, Shirley Chisholm, Eleanor Holmes Norton, and Michelle Obama. All of these women influenced me to seek elective office for different reasons but mostly because of their struggle to make things better for the common good of all human beings. For example, I admire Maxine Waters because just like myself she began her career as a public servant and teacher. She is now considered by many to be one of the most powerful women in American politics. I admire Fannie Lou Hamer for being instrumental in the fight for civil rights and voting rights. I admire Shirley Chisholm for being the first Black woman elected to Congress and first Black female candidate for president of the United States. In addition, Eleanor Holmes Norton has been a major figure in DC politics for as long as I can remember. As a Congresswoman, she has tirelessly fought for DC statehood and the right for DC to have full voting representation in Congress. Lastly, I admire Michelle Obama because I believe that she is the driving force to Barack Obama's career and presidency. She was a brilliant mentor to him when he first began his career in Chicago and I believe she is vital in a number of the decisions that he makes as he leads the country.

Q: Did you find social networking on the Internet advantageous to your campaign?

A: It was definitely an advantage to my campaign. I know that I received tons of votes just by that alone. Of course, nothing beats grassroots campaigning, holding forums, meets and greets, canvassing, and just connecting with constituents. But it was also good to have them be able to go to my website and get more information.

Q: How does running for elective office impact a female candidate's family life? Do you think that the impact is the same for male candidates?

A: Personally speaking, it affected my family in many ways. There was a definite strain put on my marriage mostly because of the lack of time in the household and my husband having to take on more responsibilities with my son.

Q: How do you think African American women would benefit from having more African American women running for elective office?

A: I think African American women would benefit because more of their concerns and interest would be addressed and not overlooked.

Q: Based on feedback you received on the campaign trail, what are the biggest concerns for African American women today?

A: Education, unemployment, housing, and programs for female recovering addicts, convicted felons, and former and current welfare recipients.

Q: How did running for elective office change your life?

A: It changed my life because now I see things on a broader level. Even though I campaigned on a local level, I see how fixing problems in our community can in turn improve things on a national and global level. I also saw the backstabbing and corruption that takes place first hand and the fact that the best candidate for the job doesn't always win.

Q: You ran your campaign in a jurisdiction that is largely African American so obviously being African American was an advantage. As a candidate in the primary, did you benefit more from being African American or being a woman?

A: I believe that I benefit more from being an African American primarily because the majority of Prince Georges County is made up residents of African American descent. It is one of the most affluent African American counties in this country.

Q: Do you think that there will ever be an African American female president?

A: Realistically, I don't think so but I'm praying that Michelle Obama will consider throwing in her bid for President some day.

Patricia Washington

Dr. Patricia Washington was a candidate for the California General Assembly in 2012 for the 79th District. Currently, she is a commissioner with the City of San Diego Human Relations Commission. She serves as the cochair of We Advocate Gender Equity (WAGE) and the cochair of the LBGT Caucus of the California Democratic Party. Dr. Washington is a former president of the San Diego Democratic Women's Club and member of the San Diego branch of the National Association for the Advancement of Colored People (NAACP). She currently serves as a director of the African American Democratic Caucus for the San Diego region. She also shared her thoughts on running for elective office, although she is veteran of electoral politics.

Q: Dr. Washington, what made you decide initially to run for office?

A: A strong belief that I would be a more suitable representative for the residents of my district than any of the other candidates who put their names forward to represent the district I live in.

I have been a community volunteer for years and have remained grounded in the belief that it is wrong for people who work full-time to be barely scraping by. I am concerned that rising health care costs make it increasingly hard for families to afford doctors' visits and know far too many people for whom the emergency room is the only place many of the residents in my area get medical care. I have worked hard to do something to address the fact that too many kids in our working-class or working-poor neighborhoods are dropping out of school, and too many of those who do graduate end up with empty diplomas that don't qualify them for college or career. I belong to organizations or support endeavors that recognize that workers are scapegoated and targeted for abuse. It concerns me that our sick or elderly too often have to choose between buying food or paying for prescription medicine.

I have been in the trenches and on the frontlines for these issues. They say that the best predictor of future behavior is past behavior. My past behavior demonstrates that I am committed to our families and communities getting the resources they need to enjoy the quality of life they deserve.

Q: What were your bi ggest obstacles during your candidacy?

A: Difficulties raising large amounts of money by the financial filing dead-lines, misrepresentations of my past and current activities, and people who inaccurately represented themselves as having talents, professional skills, and financial resources for my campaign who either didn't have them or never intended to utilize those resources on behalf of my cam-paign and false friends.

Q: Did you feel like there were certain obstacles that were specific to you being a minority candidate?

A: Yes, a part of people believing they should invest time and/or money in your campaign comes from their being able to look at you and the people who previously held the position you are seeking has to do with the race, gender and sexual orientation, stature of others who have gone before you. One elected told me that I needed to surround myself with Whites, Jewish individuals and lawyers to win.

Q: What is your background?

A: I grew up poor in southeastern Virginia. My grandmother, a domes-tic worker who could not read or write, raised me. I became a mother in the 10th grade. I would have become another statistic if not for the persistence of my third and fourth grade teachers, Ms. Newsome and Ms. Glover.
While in the third grade, they made sure I got my first pair of eye-glasses when it was clear that I was severely near-sighted.
They worked with my grandmother to provide me a solid educational foundation. Most people expected me to stay poor and dependent, because that was what most 15-year-old single mothers from my part of town did.
Ms. Newsome and Ms. Glover used the power of their positions to tear down walls of ignorance, poverty and fear of failure.
Those three women, with the help of others, got me through high school and into college. After graduating from college, I went on to re-ceive a Ph.D. and became an educator myself.

Q: Did any of your recent experiences catapult you into entering the race in the 79th district?

A: Yes, in addition to the reasons stated above, I also worked as a part of a community coalition on redistricting that helped heightened my concern that the Assembly district I am running to represent has an elected leader who will be a genuine voice for underserved com-munities.

Q: Given your recent experiences being a candidate for office, why do you think more women do not run for elective office?

A: More women don't run for office because it is extremely difficult and challenging to put your life on hold so that you can devote the hours and hours needed to find financial contributions and to garner the endorsements needed to be seen as viable for elected office. It is difficult to stomach the betrayals that repeatedly blindside you and because more and more women's organizations that were initially created to increase the number and quality of women in elected and appointed office have themselves become overly populated by women (and men) who gravitate to candidates of wealth or who are easy to manipulate for corporate or other purposes; grooming community leaders from the communities that they seek to represent is a thing of the past.

Q: Who are some of the women in politics that you admire, nationally or locally?

A: Eleanor Roosevelt (deceased), Fannie Lou Hamer (deceased) Ella Baker (deceased), Mary Salas, Hon. Mona Rios (National City Council), Mrs. Michele Obama, Ann Richards (deceased), Delores Huerta, Aurora Cudal (not in elected office).

Q: Do you find social networking on the internet advantageous to your campaign?

A: Yes.

Q: How does running for elective office impact a female candidate's family life?

A: Do you think that the impact is the same for male candidates? It has a tremendous impact. I don't believe the impact is the same for males, although I do believe the biggest gender difference is people instinctively believe it makes sense when a male candidate- regardless of prior experience or political participation-runs, but scratch their heads when a particular woman runs and wonders why she is doing it. Motivations and viability are questioned more for women than men.

Q: How do you think African American women would benefit from having more African American women running for elective office or just more women in general?

A: We need more women of highly caliber and deeper, demonstrated and unwavering commitments to underserved populations running for office, but most definitely more African American women.

Q: Based on feedback that you have received so far on the campaign trail, what are the biggest issues for African American women today?

A: Access to large amounts of money from individual donors who want to make an investment in both the candidate and the least monied constituents that the candidate intends to serve as training grounds for elected office that are truly grounded in grooming everyday citizens to run for office, the need to restore democracy into elective politics (today it's about how much money you can raise to give to companies to produce mailers, TV ads, etc. professional campaign paraphernalia) and framing issues in ways that will sell to under-informed voters, regardless of what is truly best for the community. Another challenge is the proliferation of individuals who advertise themselves as campaign professionals who are incredibly lousy at what they do who cost candidates thousands of dollars in valuable resources because they are able to trap them into contracts based on the illusion that they are political experts who have access to donors and other resources to help women candidates.

Q: Has running for elective office change your life?
A: Profoundly.

Q: As a candidate for the assembly, do you feel that you benefit more from being triple identity candidate?
A: In an ideal world I should benefit. In actuality, any and all identity benefits accrue to those with the most direct access to wealth, power and individuals who are determined to decide who can gain access.

Q: How long do you think it will be before this country elects a female president, an LGBT president, and/or an African American female president?
A: A lot less longer after President Obama gets re-elected.

Q: What role does the intersection of race, gender, and class play in electoral politics?
A: A tremendous role, White donors and elected officials (who either begin in the wealthier classes or become wealthy after being elected) still gravitate to people who make them feel comfortable or that they believe are more like themselves in interests, values, and willingness to deal away the best interests of underserved populations. As long as money (we need clean elections) rules who can be considered a serious contender and people of wealth can handpick who can move forward (regardless of what is best for the area's residents or who the average resident would prefer) in politics, the intersection of race, gender, class,

and sexual orientation will always play a heavy role in electoral politics. Money gives people the ability to manipulate kneejerk reactions to the race, gender, class, and sexual orientation of candidates in political messaging, etc. It can work for a candidate or against a candidate.

A Look Forward

In November 2005, Montgomery County, Maryland, one of the nation's largest suburban counties, elected five women to become judges in that month's elections. As a result, 6 of Montgomery County's 19 judges would be women. Local representatives termed it Montgomery county's Year of the Woman. Out of the five female judges elected there, four ran as Republicans and one ran as a Democrat. One Democrat candidate, Cheryl Austin, lost by just 356 votes. Garrett D. Paige of Abington became the county's only African American judge and only the second African American judge in the county's history. An example that demonstrates the disparity between the percentage of Black women in an electorate in comparison to the percentage of representation is in the nation's capital where Black women make up the majority of the entire voting electorate, but on a city council of 13 council members as of 2012, only *two* are Black women.

President Barack Obama, in an official proclamation declaring March as Women's History Month, he stated that America "must correct persisting inequalities" facing women in every sphere of life, such as making less money and having greater family burdens than men.[5] These burdens are particularly punitive to Black women, who are statistically more likely to be the sole breadwinners and parents in their households. Some candidates such as Donna Edwards, Congresswoman from the state of Maryland, choose to wait until their children are older before deciding to pursue elective office.

Cynthia McKinney, Pat Washington, and Julia Williams are just a few examples of the progress that is being made in promoting more African American women to elective offices. More African American women need to be encouraged and supported in their individual and collective pursuits for elective office. Usually, it is whether or not these candidates can rise through the party ranks that will most likely determine if these candidates will be able to mount successful political campaigns, particularly at the local level.

In 1972, the Black leaders met to devise strategy outside of Chicago and to discuss political options for the upcoming presidential election. An anonymous source had reported the following being said at that strategy meeting in regards to Chisholm: "In this first serious effort of Blacks for High political office, it would be better if it were a man."[6] The statement would symbolize the unspoken thoughts of individuals during that time period in regards to a Black woman's candidacy for president.

African American women's history is mired with both racial oppression and gender subordination. African American women desire the fulfillment of all rights and privileges therein of both their race and their gender. There must be a working dialogue between the various ethnicities of women in progressive feminist organizations regardless of the race and class issues that must also be engaged enacted upon. Feminist organizations must share leadership with African American women and make tangible strides in integrating their organizations. The goal must be to strive for a collective cessation of gender oppression for all women.

There are different expectations for women who seek elective office, regardless of color. Many women of color lack the exposure and visibility necessary to successfully run for elective office, particularly as novices. Oftentimes they lack the resources, including financial resources, needed to mount a campaign to successfully attain an elective office. There must be stronger and more effective drives to recruit more candidates that will appeal to the demographic of African American women. The difference in voter participation between married and unmarried women continues to have an increasing influence in election results, with unmarried women representing the largest block at 28 percent.[7]

Shirley Chisholm, Black feminist icon, remarked: "When I die, I want to be remembered as a woman who lived in the 20th century and who dared to be a catalyst of change. I don't want to be remembered as the first black woman who went to Congress. And I don't even want to be remembered as the first woman who happened to be black to make the bid for the presidency. I want to be remembered as a woman who fought for change in the 20th century. That's what I want."[8]

Black Conservatism

African Americans had traditionally voted Republican from the days of President Abraham Lincoln and the late 19th century when most Blacks identified themselves as supporters of the Republican Party. Many Blacks shifted their political alliance to the Democratic Party during the presidency of Franklin Roosevelt after finding Roosevelt's policies and programs advantageous to their communities. This shift was solidified during the Kennedy administration due in large part to the administration's commitment to civil rights, despite the fact that numerous Democratic Congressmen did not vote for the passage of the 1964 Civil Rights Act. As far as the issue of civil rights was concerned, regional lines were more important than party lines. The locality where legislators were more often than not determined their positions on civil rights issues. The Democratic Party had a major base in the South, and many southern voters were prosegregation and anti–civil rights. However, there were many Northern liberals in the Democratic Party, most notably Hubert Humphrey of Minnesota, who were pro–civil rights, so a number of Southern Democrats begin to split from the Democratic Party, such as Strom Thurmond and George Wallace, and began to run as third party Dixiecrats. The significant Democratic base in the South was slipping. Since Nixon inaugurated the Southern strategy to switch White Southerners unhappy with civil rights legislation to the Republican Party, the party has consistently acted against the aspirations of Black Americans. Part of Nixon's law and order platform was to take a more moderate position on civil rights. While this helped him win in the South and throughout the country, it turned off many minority voters, not just Blacks, and following that, most Black voters tend to vote for Democrats. The Democratic Party espouses more policies and programs geared toward the impoverished and the working class and since a disproportionate number of African Americans live below the poverty line, they tend to vote significantly more for Democratic Party candidates for elective office.

Black conservatives support for a strong national defense is oftentimes at odds with many African Americans who perceive war as a method by which our young men and women are killed for what they deem are unjust causes. Black people who are beneficiaries of government support will reject the notions of those who continually call for the lessening of government programs. Two Republican presidential candidates, Ronald Reagan and George H. W. Bush, gained less than 15 percent of Black votes.[9]

Booker T. Washington is considered to be the father of Black Conservatism. His philosophy was termed by some as accommodationism. Rightwing conservatism, however, derailed the ambitions of many civil rights era upwardly mobile Blacks. Supreme Court judge Clarence Thomas is probably the most publicly acknowledged Black conservative today.

Members of the Republican Party have vetoed civil rights legislation. Many Black conservatives support the death penalty, school vouchers, small government, and advocate for the expansion of the free market system.

They usually oppose affirmative action programs, abortion rights, and same sex marriage, as well as other issues important to African American women voters. In 2012, Republican Party presidential candidate Rick Santorum was quoted as saying that he did not want to "make Black people's lives better by giving them somebody else's money."[10] Another Republican Party presidential candidate, former House Speaker Newt Gingrich, was himself quoted as saying "African Americans should demand paychecks and not be satisfied with food stamps."[11]

There exist differing points of view on the causes of stagnation of Black progress. There has been no Black conservative movement that has garnered a lot of momentum mainly due to the stereotype surrounding Black conservatism. Many Black conservatists are often viewed negatively as being sellouts to the race for supporting certain platforms that have been viewed as contrary to the mainstream of Black America.

One recent example of was when voters from the state of Maryland were given a choice between Ben Cardin, the Democrat Party candidate for the U.S. Senate and Michael Steele, the African American candidate for the Republican Party, the majority of the African American vote went to Ben Cardin, the ultimate winner of that Maryland Senate race.

In 2010, 32 African American candidates were running for Congress in the Republican Party. It is an indication of the outreach efforts being made by the Republican Party to add diversity to the party. However, it seems that Black conservatives in general are poorly perceived and received within the African American community. Given, if a candidate is a Republican, then they can't automatically be deemed a conservative. There are differing political perspectives within the Republican Party. Many Black conservative positions on social issues put them squarely at odds with many within the Black community. Conservatives are often seen as apologists for White racism and they are often not well-received within mainstream Black America. This has an impact on the perceptions of the Republican Party as well as Black conservatism by many African American voters.

Conclusion

The African American female vote became a game changer in the 2008 presidential election and is poised to continue to be a part of the transformation of the electoral landscape in 2012.[1] During the 2008 presidential election, African American women had the highest turnout among any demographic in the United States.[2] Over 97 percent of these African American female voters voted for Barack Obama. His election to the presidency was catapulted by a large African American voter turnout, especially in Southern states such as North Carolina, South Carolina, and the Commonwealth of Virginia. African American women voted overwhelmingly for Obama, and they helped him carry states with a high percentage of African American voters, including Maryland, Louisiana, and Alabama. African Americans voted nearly unanimously to elect Barack Obama president of the United States.[3] The three largest ethnic groups in the country—African Americans, Latinos, and Asians—voted in the 2008 presidential election in unprecedented numbers.[4]

The unprecedented increase in African American voter participation in the 2008 election was mainly attributed to younger African American voters and African American female voters.[5] African American female voter participation increased by 5 percentage points. I went from 63.7 percent in the 2004 presidential election to 68.8 percent in the 2008 presidential election.[6] Amongst all racial and gender groups, African American women had the highest voter turnout for the first time ever in a presidential election.[7] Increases in Black voter turnout was most significant in states with larger African American eligible voter populations. States such as Mississippi, North Carolina, and Georgia had larger voter turnout percentages on Election Day. There was also an increase in Black voter turnout in the District of Columbia. In 2008, African American women made up only six percent of the American population.[8] Seventy-two percent of these women were unmarried.[9] African

American unmarried women had the highest voter turnout rate among all unmarried women in the 2004 presidential election.[10]

Despite lingering complaints regarding the selections of major female candidates, many see the presidential election of 2008 as a huge step in the right direction. It gave women in general a better sense of seeing themselves in positions of power in this country. Some cite the high profile of Michelle Obama as first lady as proof of this. In fact, many believe that having Michelle Obama as first lady had more of an impact on African American women than Clinton and Palin running for national office. In a nationwide survey, 8 out of 10 Black women responded that they personally identify with Michelle Obama.[11] Having Michelle Obama as first lady of the country has positively raised the profile of Black women. Among Black women, 9 in 10 also responded in the survey that Michelle Obama understands their problems and shares their values, compared to about 6 in 10 White women.[12] For many, however, the 2008 presidential campaign was not so much about gender but more about who would best be able to lead the nation.

One may ask, what was the impact of having two prominent Caucasian women run for president and vice president have for African American women? It was an amazing accomplishment, but some observers felt it did not directly represent the plight of Black women. Black women felt that even though Clinton and Palin are women, they didn't necessarily represent the specific interests of Black women. Many of the interests of Black women are mired in socioeconomic concerns that oftentimes intersect with issues of race and gender.

The impact of having Hillary Clinton become the most successful female presidential candidate in our nation's history was a substantial feat for women in general. The fact is that millions of women and men of all ages and ethnicities—including African Americans—supported the candidacy of Hillary Clinton. In fact, Hispanic women voted for Hillary Clinton in the state of New York by a 52-point margin and 32-point margin in New Jersey. Clinton far surpassed Shirley Chisholm's number of delegates that Chisholm received in her 1972 presidential run. Previous to Clinton, Chisholm formerly held the record for the largest number of delegates earned by a female candidate for the presidency. Clinton garnered 17 million votes during her quest for the presidency—the most for any female candidate for president in American history.

When Hillary Clinton delivered her concession speech on June 7, 2008, at the National Building Museum in Washington, DC, she spoke to the historic nature of both her campaign and that of Barack Obama. During this poignant speech, she made the following statement: "Children today will grow up taking for granted that an African American or a woman can, yes, become the president of the United States."[13] There were women and men of many different ethnicities and nationalities, ages, and creeds who were there to show their support of her historic candidacy. Some cried but many cheered on as witnesses to the monumental achievement that was being made by the most successful female candidate in American electoral history, who would go on to throw her support to the Democratic Party nominee, Barack Obama.

New doors were definitely opened for women and for African Americans during the groundbreaking presidential campaign of 2008, although assumptions have been made that the country is a longer way off from having an African American female president than having a White female president. The election of Barack Obama was both a political and cultural milestone for America. This relatively unknown to the national stage shocked the world by trailblazing his way to the White House. Many a person of African heritage watched on with immense pride as he was inaugurated president of the United States of America on January 20, 2009. The descendants of the people that were held in slavery were thrilled by a feat that most never thought that they would witness in their lifetimes. Obama was a master at getting blocs of African Americans and younger voters to turn up at the polls to cast their votes, which was an important factor in his victory in the 2008 presidential election.

For decades, Black voters have been chastised for allowing their votes to be taken for granted in the electoral atmosphere. The day is on the horizon where we will undoubtedly see two women on the same presidential ticket. It may be just a little later than that when we will see two women of color on the very same presidential ticket of a major political party together. Cynthia McKinney and Rosa Clemente, two women of color, ran for president and vice president on the Green Party ticket in 2008.

Moreover, one can reach the conclusion that the overwhelming majority of voters vote for who they decide the best candidate is for that particular office. Voters don't vote for candidates simply based on identity politics, in most instances. In many instances however, race will trump gender. Black women respondents, overall, feel more impacted by their race than by their gender. They generally select candidates to vote for whose platforms are in line with the issues that concern them as voters the most. If a candidate's platform addresses issues that are specific to race, they will trump some women's issues in the minds of Black women. Critical issues for the core constituency of Black women are subject to change based upon the variables of class determinations and socioeconomic status. As previously noted, unmarried Black women had the highest voter turnout rate among all unmarried women in 2004.[14] These women are oftentimes likely to be raising children so their primary issues of concern include health care, child care, education, and other issues that relate to their economic anxiety. The Lily Ledbetter Act of 2009, put forth by the 111th Congress and signed into law by President Barack Obama, restores equal protection for pay discrimination. The law will make it easier for women to fight for equal pay. According to Lake Research Partners, 34 percent of unmarried African American women feel that the federal government should do everything that it can to improve the standard of living of all poor Americans, and 22 percent of unmarried women who are not Black shared the same view. Also noted was that unmarried Black women vote more than any other unmarried group.[15]

To date, there have been 42 women of color that have served in the U.S. Congress. This number includes 28 African American women, 8 Latinas, and 6 Asian American women.[16] Shirley Chisholm and Carol Moseley Braun were the African American female pioneers in Congress as was Patsy Takemoto Mink of Hawaii, an Asian American woman who served from 1965 to 1977. Judy Chu became the first Chinese American to serve in Congress in 2009. Ileana Ros-Lehtinen, Republican from Florida, was the first Cuban American and the first Latina female ever elected to Congress.

Women are reaching a level of prominence that they never have before in electoral politics. Women were at the forefront of the national political arena in 2008. That historic presidential campaign cycle broke barriers in the male-dominated sphere of presidential politics. Many women, African American and otherwise, felt encouraged and empowered from the successes of both Hillary Clinton and Sarah Palin. After all, women still comprise the majority of voters in the United States. It was progress for women in the American political mainstream.

Many Black women claim not to connect with the feminism of the past. Many of them have at times associated feminism with White, upper class Ivy League women. There was the perception that mainstream feminism only addressed issues of middle-class White women. All women must work toward more inclusiveness and diversity within and outside of the realm of feminist issues, regardless of race or ethnicity by working toward it— together. There is power in numbers.

It is becoming more and more obvious that African American women are emerging as a more influential voting bloc than ever before. According to the Joint Center for Economic and Political Studies, in the 2008 presidential election, African Americans represented 20 percent of the electorate in the Commonwealth of Virginia. In the November 2009 gubernatorial election, their representation went down to 15 percent and Republican Bob McDonnell was elected governor.

One Black female voter, responding to a NOAW poll, stated the following regarding the 2008 presidential election: "It made me feel like I have a chance if I go in that direction." That thought will certainly become more commonplace as time moves on and more progress continues to be made for women and minorities in electoral politics. The trend was demonstrated with a new crop of African American leaders that were elected to national and state offices throughout the country during the 2010 midterm elections. America would vote for a Black man for president in larger numbers than they would vote for a woman in the 2008 Democratic presidential primary. This is a major indication of the progress made regarding the nation's past racial divide. In Fort Pierce, Florida, in 2012 the city is poised to elect either the city's first Black mayor or the city's first female mayor. Since 1980, no Black or female candidates had been successful in their bids for the mayorship in Fort Pierce.[17] The makeup of the city is approximately 39.7 percent African American and 39.3 percent White.[18] Neither race nor gender seems to be the cornerstone of the upcoming local election there.

Afterword

Between the years 1777 and 1807, women in the United States who could vote in several states during that time slowly and systematically lost the right to vote. In 1870, the Fifteenth Amendment to the U.S. Constitution guaranteed citizens the right to vote, but not women of any race, including African American women. For the first time, with the ratification of the Fourteenth Amendment to the Constitution, women of all races were excluded in the Constitution from full citizenship in regards to voting. In 1893, New Zealand was noted as the first country to give women the right to vote. For 72 years from the first women's rights convention in Seneca Falls, New York, the citizens of America, both men and women and numerous ethnicities, fought for women's right to vote. The United States followed New Zealand in the year 1920 by granting all women the right to vote. In 1923, the National Women's Party proposed the Equal Rights Amendment with the goal of eradicating gender discrimination. The amendment was never ratified. There was almost a century between the election of Joseph Hayne Rainey, Republican from South Carolina, in 1870, the first free Black man elected to the House of Representatives, and the year that the first Black woman was elected to Congress, Democrat Party candidate Shirley Chisholm in 1968. Shirley Chisholm would eventually become the first African American woman or man to run for president from a major political party.

Black women were the backbone of the civil rights movement as the leadership in the forefront was mainly relegated to the men. The discrimination of women within the civil rights movement was typical of its time. Black women should have had a separate movement from the civil rights movement and the women's right movement because they were secondary in both movements. The Black women who participated in these movements were not just history makers; they were pioneers who broke down barriers during some of the most tumultuous times in our nation's past. Following the civil rights movement, Ella Baker would go on to become a candidate of the New York City Council in the Liberal Party. As a result of the heroic efforts of Fannie Lou Hamer and countless others, the Democratic Party would eventually rewrite its delegate rules to include minorities and women.

Many Black women were active during the Antebellum period as both abolitionists and suffragists. As Black women worked alongside White women in the National Women's Suffrage Association, Southern White women in the group advocated for the enfranchisement of only White women. Noted African American female leaders such as Mary Church Terrell, Ana Julia Cooper, and Josephine St. Pierre Ruffin emerged out of this movement. The Nineteenth Amendment, which granted women, including Black women, the right to vote, was signed into law by Secretary of State Bainbridge Colby on August 26, 1920.

The major focus of the feminist movement was on sexism, not racism. Many have suggested that feminism was created to put White women on equal footing with White men. Critics have charged such things that modern-day feminism has demeaned the status of motherhood and that women who advocate for the feminist doctrine are trying to be men. The truth however is that feminism includes various perspectives on social and political phenomena. Thousands of Black women have benefitted from the doors that have been opened as a result of the positive actions of the feminist movement. Women have more earning potential than ever before and currently hold positions of power that women decades ago could only dream about.

Following emancipation, the Great Black Migration proved to forever alter the landscape of Black electoral participation. Millions of Blacks moved to northern cities looking for opportunity and a better way of life. During this time, most African Americans were self-identified as Republicans. There was a huge shift to the Democratic Party during the era of Franklin Delano Roosevelt. President Roosevelt, a Democrat, and his New Deal programs and his Black cabinet won the support of millions of Black voters. The Voting Rights Act, signed by President Lyndon B. Johnson in 1965, made a huge difference in increasing Black voter participation by outlawing the unfair practices that discriminated against Black voters and also establishing more Black districts. Prior to the passage of the Voting Rights Act, there had been widespread disenfranchisement of African Americans throughout the United States, particularly in the South.

Within four years of its passage, voter registration in the South doubled. Shifts in demographics changed the Black political base. In 1965, there were about 100 elected officials in the United States; today there are over 7,000.[1] The Act increased Black voter registration in the short term. It also led to the formation of more majority Black districts in the nation. The Voting Rights Act was a necessary intervention to alleviate the disenfranchisement of Black voters. The landmark civil rights legislation has been a conduit to the continuing political empowerment of African American voters. Countless Americans died to guarantee the right to vote to all of America's citizens. Not only is voting a privilege and an inherent right, it is also a responsibility. Through that voting power, voters have the responsibility to vote and vote for candidates who will best represent their stand on critical issues and matters of concern. Nineteenth-century African American representatives in Congress were primarily Republican. There was a realignment of African American voters beginning in the Great Depression era. This trend began to change around the era of the New Deal reforms. Up to the 1940s, only one African American member served at any time in Congress. It wasn't until 1955 that no more than two would serve simultaneously. There would only be 13 African Americans elected to Congress between 1929 and 1970, none of these being African American women.

Although the United States has yet to select a woman as its national leader, Hillary Clinton took the country toward a huge step in that direction with her historic campaign for the Democratic nomination for president in 2008. She was strong in the face of adversity, displaying vigilance and perseverance. She showed that a woman could indeed stand her ground in what had been relatively a man's domain in politics. She started off her campaign as the presumed frontrunner that was forced to acquiesce to a young, dynamic newcomer to the national spotlight. Hillary Clinton won more primaries and delegates than any other female candidate in history, normalizing the idea that a woman can indeed be a serious candidate for the presidency of the United States. No woman has yet to be nominated by a major political party for president in the United States. Hillary Clinton's candidacy helped to make this a less difficult obstacle for other women to overcome.

Barack Obama was truly a dynamic presidential candidate. He was a great motivational speaker whose message resonated with millions of Americans of all persuasions. Once Obama won the Iowa caucus, African Americans grew to believe and conceive that yes, this great nation would elect a Black man as its executive leader. Obama dared us to hope and slowly, yet powerfully, his message caught on. His campaign was a symbol of hope to many, not only in America, but around the world. What his victory meant to the descendants of slaves in America is immeasurable. When he was finally announced as the winner of the presidential election on November 4, 2008, 359 years after the first African slaves were brought to the Americas, the people rejoiced like never before. One could hear their neighbors scream, and others fell out into the streets onto their knees screaming, "Thank You Lord! Thank You!" One elder remarked, "I never thought that I'd see the day where America would elect a Black president in my lifetime." His election was the culmination of centuries of involuntary servitude, oppression, discrimination, exclusion, and finally triumph for millions of Americans. Black voter turnout in the 2008 election that made Barack Obama president of the United States of America was at its highest point ever in this nation's history. Black voters were determined to have a dramatic impact on that election and with their record-high turnout, which is exactly what they collectively did.

The 2010 Midterm Elections

Some analysts had predicted that a strong showing from African American voters during the 2010 midterm elections could influence the results of numerous Senate, House, and gubernatorial races. Overall, Black turnout was low for the 2010 midterm elections in several key states such as Florida. There was strong African American voter turnout in California, Delaware, and New York, states that also produced strong Democratic Party wins.[2] African American voter turnout was smaller than in the 2008 presidential election even though most analysts agree that it is difficult to compare presidential election turnouts to midterm election turnouts. The 2008 presidential election was unique, given that it was the first election to have an African American candidate from a major political party.

Increases in Black voter turnout in Nevada helped to secure the re-election of Senate majority leader Harry Reid in 2010. Black voter turnout was also particularly strong in Ohio and Illinois. Democratic gubernatorial candidate, Pat Quinn, was the recipient of a strong Black voter turnout and was able to win his race in Illinois.

Overall, Black voter turnout was not sufficient enough to change many election outcomes. Lower Black turnout at the polls may have had a profound effect on the 2010 midterm election outcomes. Democratic candidates ended up losing 60 seats in the House of Representatives. More than 12 of these states represented districts with high numbers of Black voters. States such as Virginia, North Carolina, and Indiana that President Obama won in 2008 in many cases elected Republican candidates. Nationally, 90 percent of Black voters supported Democratic House candidates compared to 10 percent of Black voters who voted for Republican House candidates.[3] There was a gender gap between Black men and Black women with 93 percent of Black women supporting Democratic House candidates and 6 percent supporting Republican House candidates and 84 percent of Black men voting for Democratic House candidates and 14 percent of Black men voting for Republican House candidates.[4]

In terms of African Americans elected to office in 2010, Massachusetts governor Deval Patrick was re-elected governor of that state, which was a first for an African American. Chip Flowers became the first African American to win statewide office in Delaware, where he was elected the state treasurer. Anthony Brown was re-elected as the lieutenant governor of the state of Maryland in the 2010 midterm elections. As a result of the midterm elections, there will be 44 African American members in the 112th Congress, a historic high. This includes two new Black Republicans in the House of Representatives, Tim Scott of South Carolina and Allen West of Florida.

There were also some gains for African American women in the 2010 midterm elections. Terri Sewell, a Harvard University and Princeton University graduate, became the first Black woman elected to Congress from the state of Alabama in the 7th Congressional district. Sewell is a partner in a law firm who was able to parlay her community activism into a successful campaign that led her into the halls of Congress. Jennifer Carroll was elected the lieutenant governor of the state of Florida as a Republican Party candidate. She is a veteran of the Navy and in 2003 became the first Black woman to be elected to the Florida state legislature as a Republican following two unsuccessful bids. In California, there was a clean sweep of the eight statewide offices for Democratic candidates in California. Kamala Harris, the district attorney of San Francisco, was elected the first female African American and the first Indian American attorney general in the state of California. She was elected in a close race against Republican Party candidate and Los Angeles District Attorney Steve Cooley. The race was so close that it took three weeks following the election to determine a winner.

In contrast, former Washington, DC, mayor Adrian Fenty turned off many of the African American women in his city by publicly snubbing two prominent Black women, including the late Dorothy I. Height, a former national president of the National Council of Negro Women. Three weeks prior to the District of Columbia Democratic primary, his approval rating with Black women was at a dismally low percentage. *Washington Post* writer Courtland Milloy posed the question: "How did D.C. Mayor Adrian M. Fenty lose the love of so many black women—the most faithful and forgiving constituents a black man in public office can have?"[5] Fenty went on to lose the Democratic mayoral primary to District of Columbia Council chairman, Vincent C. Gray. Fenty lost large numbers of Black votes.[6] Gray won with 53 percent of the vote to Fenty's 46 percent, with all but 15 precincts counted. Undoubtedly, losing the support of many Black voters, including Black women, is the reason for the incumbent mayor's loss at the polls.

Democratic Party candidates can get the plurality of African American votes but they still must focus on getting high Black voter turnout on Election Day, due to the inconsistent apathy of many African American voters. It is estimated that the Democratic National Committee spent upwards of $3 million on Black voter outreach for the 2010 midterm elections. It would take an awful lot to alienate Blacks from the Democratic base as recent trends have demonstrated. The complexities of racial issues make it problematic for most African Americans it seems to join the Republican Party, given that there are currently only two major political parties in the country. The past contemptible views of some Southern conservatives serve as a continuous obstacle that unfortunately still resonates for many African American voters. It is estimated that a little more than 10 percent of African American voters support Republican Party candidates. The Republican Party did however attempt to appeal to Black voters by nominating 14 Black candidates across the country for offices during the 2010 midterm elections. Perhaps if the Democratic Party was able to mobilize a stronger Black turnout, the party could have reduced their losses in the 2010 midterm elections. Additionally, the conservative mantra is manifesting a new look for feminism. Several Republican Party female candidates who were profiled nationally during the recent midterm elections included Carly Fiorina and Meg Whitman in California races, Sharon Angle in Nevada, and Christine O'Donnell in Delaware.

African Americans have in the past been deprived of ample and feasible opportunities to participate fully in the political process. As a voting bloc, African American voters have shown to be a decisive factor in some close national and state elections. African American women must grasp the full impact of their political decisions. Access equals power. More access to political platforms results in more power to affect the overall decision-making and law-making processes. Black women must strive even harder to be a central segment of the political domain. Many African American women do not know their real potential to wield political power. They feel too often that when they fight for their identities as women that they are somehow being traitors to Black men. These prevailing cultural misconceptions are an additional hurdle to the political aspirations of too many Black women.

In addition, first lady Michelle Obama is arguably the most powerful Black woman in American politics today. Due to her popularity and impact as an effective campaigner, Mrs. Obama was dispatched to campaign for Democratic Party candidates across the nation during the 2010 midterm elections. But Mrs. Obama is *not* an elected official. Her appeal to voters, however, helped to influence the balance of power in Washington during the 2010 midterm elections. Three generations of Black females currently reside in 1600 Pennsylvania Avenue due in large part to the leadership, sacrifice, and appeal of Michelle Obama.

As of 2011, there are 41 members of the U.S. Congress that are Black males, compared to 15 members being Black women. There are two Black males who serve as governor or lieutenant governor of a state, compared to one Black female lieutenant governor nationwide. As of 2010, 4.5 percent of Black men are in state legislatures compared to 2.7 percent of Black females.[7] There were 618 Black men who served as county officials nationwide compared to 139 for Black women and Black men are nearly double the number of municipal officials than Black women in 2010. There are similar trends in the both the Asian and Latino communities as well.

Seventeen of the Democratic nominees for House seats were African American women and more were victorious than ever before.[8] Having more Black women in public office is more than an achievable goal. More Black women must seek elective office. They must be courageous and more optimistic as they embark on their pursuits for public offices on all levels. Black women won't attain public offices unless they first become *candidates* for public offices. There are still lots of inequalities in electoral politics. For instance, the Commonwealth of Virginia has elected only one African American, Representative Bobby Scott, to the House of Representatives since Reconstruction. In order to better affect issues in our communities, Black women must be an active part of the decision-making procedural bodies. They must attain key positioning to effectively voice concerns and to address said concerns, some of which are specific to the quality of life for Black women and their families. They must be in a more advantageous decision-making capacity in executive and legislative capacities to cover mandates and the important issues of local and state services, quality of life debates, and fiscal issues. If you would enjoy contributing to the greater good, then you have a responsibility to be an active and involved participant in the political process period. Becoming a candidate for public office is a noble mission and one in which one person can ultimately improve the lives of many. For many citizens, being a public officeholder is one of the best vehicles for positive change in their communities.

A 2010 survey conducted by the National Organization for African American women determined that the most pressing issue for Black women in 2010 according to respondents was as follows: 36 percent of respondents answered that leading single-income households as the most pressing issue for Black women followed by 27 percent of respondents who listed AIDS as the most pressing problem for Black women and 14 percent who listed workplace disparities and the lack of female elective officials respectively as the most pressing problem. Black female voters care passionately about a multitude of quality of life issues, which include but are not limited to education, jobs, and health care, as do many Americans. Black women want what everyone else wants: Black women want good schools in their neighborhoods; they want to raise their children in safe communities. They need strong voices to represent the issues that matter most to all of us in legislative, judicial, and executive bodies.

The lingering issue concerning the lack of Black female officeholders nationwide must be addressed. Statistically, Black women are more likely to be the heads of their households so they in effect have fewer resources and networks to mount successful campaigns in pursuit of public office. In order to have more Black female candidates for elective office, better and more comprehensive strategies need to be developed to encourage the ambitions of Black women to run for public office. An anonymous NOAW survey asking Black women what would discourage them from running for office offered that many Black women are hindered by what they feel may be a public fallout from past actions or indiscretions as well as issues such as child care and lack of adequate networks. A candidate's ability to appeal to specific groups of voters in today's changing American electorate is crucial. Voters are more likely to support candidates who are visible in their neighborhoods. They are receptive to candidates who reach across the aisles to make them feel valued and listened to. They vote for candidates who are like them. Issues that are important to women voters were prominent in the 2008 presidential campaign.

Black female candidates are too often dismissed by both male and female voters for a myriad of reasons. Many, many Black women have immense amounts of talent and expertise that can be utilized quite effectively in various positions of elective office on the local, state, and national level. Shirley Chisholm pointed out in her book *Unbought and Unbossed* that tremendous amounts of talent are lost by society because that talent wears a skirt. Many potential candidates for elective office can't or don't desire to deal with the sometimes cumbersome mechanics of politics nor do they desire to play the inside games of politics.

More Black woman should be recruited to run for elective office by their respective political parties on the local level and they need support with the cumbersome tasks of campaign fundraising, field operations, and candidate education and preparation. There is a lot of truth in the adage, "All politics are local." More candidates have to be drafted at the local level. The Center for Women in American Politics touts a program that is designated to train more women of color to run for public office. This program provides excellent opportunities for potential female candidates of color to receive training and education which includes advice and support from veteran, current and former public officeholders and political party leaders.[9]

According to David Bositis of the Joint Center for Political and Economic Studies, Black voters have made some difference in the electoral atmosphere. Having analyzed the African American electorate for more than two decades, Bositis says that Black voters have changed the politics of particular states. When asked what impact African American female voters had on the 2008 presidential election, Bositis observes that Obama would not have won several states without the Black female vote. He does however state that Black female voters cannot by themselves be a powerful voting bloc, but this would be the case for most groups since Black women only represent seven or eight percent of the voting population but they still are an important part of the overall electorate. Dr. Bositis, the nation's foremost expert on the African American electorate, cites election laws as a factor that inhibits more African American women from being elected to office. Bositis sees the election of Kamala Harris as the state attorney general in California as a key gain for women of color in elective office since she will now be in a good alignment to make a possible future run for the governorship. No African American woman has ever been elected governor of any state.

The Black vote has in the recent past been a great asset to the Democratic Party in increasing their majorities in both chambers of Congress. The Democrats have also won key governorships as a result of the votes from one of their most loyal voting blocs, the African American electorate. Again, African American women make up the majority of the African American electorate. Political parties must be encouraged toward how advantageous it will be to make more Black women a more central part of their parties' nomination process. There are hundreds of local elections where the votes of Black women determine the election outcomes. Black women play a large role in driving the votes for the Black community. These parties must find appropriate ways of addressing the lack of both Black and female elected officials nationwide. Given the current structure of our political system, novices to electoral politics would have to be assisted more by these parties to successfully jump over the hurdle of incumbency. Incumbents are statistically more likely to win more elections than their challengers.

There have only been six African American members of the U.S. Senate in our nation's history. Hiram Rhodes Revels was the first in 1870. He was followed by Blanche Kelso Bruce and Edward William Brooke, III, the first Black senator to be re-elected to the Senate. Carol Moseley Braun became the first African American female senator to serve in 1992. Barack Obama was elected to the Senate in 2004 and left the Senate to become the president of the United States. Roland Burris was appointed to finish Obama's term until November 2010. Burris, the great-grandson of an African American slave, remarked upon the end of his term, "I am today the only Black American member of this Senate . . . when the one 112th Congress is sworn in this coming January, there will not be a single Black American who takes the oath of office in this chamber. This is simply unacceptable."[10] Burris was being replaced by the winner of the election to fill the remainder of Burris's term and a full term of six years, Republican candidate Mark Kirk. Burris's exit leaves the Senate with no African American members.

A reenergized Black electorate can be developed just by getting more African Americans into elective offices. As African Americans pursue what is most politically beneficial to them, there will undoubtedly continue to be shifts in voter participation and perhaps even party affiliations. Political parties must also play a more proactive role in recruiting more diverse candidates for elective office. As a community, many African Americans have not fully taken into full account the necessary task of campaign fundraising and this is often an extremely difficult task for many minority women who pursue public office.

The first Black American to serve in Congress was Hiram Revels of the state of Mississippi, who began his service in the Senate on February 25, 1870. Joseph Rainey of South Carolina was the first African American elected to serve in Congress in December of 1870. These members were confronted with a segregated institution that followed the segregated policies of the city where it was contained. The first African American popularly elected to the Senate was Edward Brook of Massachusetts in 1966. Two years later, Shirley Chisholm became the first Black woman elected to Congress from New York. In 1992, Carol Moseley Braun of Illinois was the first Black woman elected to serve in the U.S. Senate. In 2010, there were 9.2 percent of the members of the U.S. House of Representative were African American, compared to no African American members in the U.S. Senate.[11] Blacks held three percent of governor and lieutenant governorships and they represented 7.2 percent of statewide legislative positions.[12] Since 1971, only one-fourth of the Congressional Black caucus chairmen have been women (6 out of 24—Yvonne Braithewaite Burke, Cardiss Collins, Maxine Waters, Eddie Bernice Johnson, Carolyn Cheeks Kilpatrick, and Barbara Lee). Shirley Chisholm served as the secretary of the 95th and 96th Congress' Democratic caucus. Maxine Waters served as the chief deputy whip of the Democratic caucus of the 106th, 107th, 108th, 109th, and 110th Congresses.

The Gender and Multicultural Leadership Project, a national study of the nation's political arena with a specific focus on race and gender, has determined that Black men continue to outnumber Black women in elective office nationwide. For this reason, among others, more Black women must come forward as candidates for office to effect more positive change within all of our communities so that tomorrow's crop of Black female leaders can emerge and do justice to the awesome legacy that has been passed to them. Black women should continue to be an important part of voter participation, protection, and voter education efforts. The increase in the diversity of electoral politics must continue for the benefit of all.

America has always been a multiethnic society. We have and must continue to strive for a truly representative democracy that is more inclusive of all races and genders. More Black women could win elective offices by utilizing multiracial and multigender coalitions and voting blocs, given the changing demographic shifts in the nation's electorate. The racial barriers have been shattered, now on to the prevailing gender barriers. Young Black boys can now declare with certainty that they can indeed become president of the United States. The question remains, can young Black girls, or any girl for that matter, say the same? The feminist consciousness is not as strong as it could be for many African American women, but there are indications that the dynamic is changing. Black women must have their own voices within the political spectrum. In the historic words of civil rights and feminist pioneer Shirley Chisholm, "I am Black and I am a woman." As Black women, we are clearly defined by both of our identities, our racial identity *and* our gender identity. Our two identities are both distinct and vital to the ongoing struggle for equality and fairness. Outside of that, our identities don't define our entirety. African American female candidates don't desire to be elected just because they are Black or because they are female. Regardless of race and gender politics, we must continue to attract viable and effective candidates for elective office. Female candidates for elective office are no longer merely making symbolic bids for office; they are making substantive ones as well. These candidates, if elected, will be expected to deliver economic and political benefits to their constituents. The more minority female candidates that are elected to office, the more accessible the political process will become to them and it will be more favorable to their overall legislative interests within the existing power structure. The positioning of African American women within the American political landscape will continue to strengthen the social, economic, and political empowerment of all women and minorities. African American political pioneer Shirley Chisholm stated it best:

> When I die, I want to be remembered as a woman who lived in the 20th century and who dared to be a catalyst of change. I don't want to be remembered as the first black woman who went to Congress. And I don't even want to be remembered as the first woman who happened to be black to make the bid for the presidency. I want to be remembered as a woman who fought for change in the 20th century. That's what I want.

African American Women in American Electoral Politics: Major Milestones

- Charlotta Bass became the first African American woman to run for vice president when she was nominated by the Progressive Party in 1952.
- Shirley Chisholm became the first African American female elected to Congress in 1968. She was elected to represent the state of New York.

- Shirley Chisholm became the first African American, male or female, to run for president in a major political party in 1972.
- Barbara Jordan became the first African American woman elected to the U.S. Congress from the Deep South representing the state of Texas in 1972.
- Yvonne Brathwaite Burke was the first African American woman elected to the U.S. House of Representatives from a western state when she was elected from the state of California. Burke would eventually become the first female chair of the Congressional Black caucus.
- Barbara Jordan became the first African American woman to deliver a keynote address at a major party political convention during the Democratic National Convention in 1976.
- Lenora Fulani became the first African American and the first female candidate to get on the presidential ballot in all 50 states in 1988.
- Sharon Pratt Dixon became the first African American woman to serve as mayor of a major American city when she was elected mayor of the District of Columbia in 1991.
- Carol Moseley Braun became the first African American woman elected to the U.S. Senate in 1992.
- Stephanie Tubbs Jones became the first African American woman to chair a congressional committee when she chaired the House Committee on Ethics in 2007.
- Cynthia McKinney accepted the Green Party presidential nomination on July 13, 2008.
- Donna Edwards became the first African American woman to represent the state of Maryland in the U.S. Congress in 2008.
- Karen Bass became the first African American woman to become speaker of a state assembly when she became speaker of the California State Assembly in May 2008.
- Kamala Harris became the first woman, the first African American and the first Indian American to be elected attorney general in the state of California in November 2010.
- Jennifer Carroll became the first African American woman to be elected lieutenant governor of the state of Florida in 2010.
- Terri Sewell became the first African American woman to be elected to the U.S. Congress from the state of Alabama in 2010.

Notes

Chapter 1 Cohesive Representation

1. Center for American Women and Politics, http://cawp.rutgers.edu/, accessed May 29, 2011.

2. Ibid.

3. "The History of Slavery in America," Slavery in America, http://slaveryin america.org/history/overview.htm, accessed May 30, 2011.

4. Claire Cohen, "Breakdown of Demographics Reveals How Black Voters Swept Obama into the White House," *Mail Online*, http://www.dailymail.co.uk/ news/worldnews/article-1083335, accessed November 5, 2008.

5. Center for American Women and Politics.

6. Ibid.

7. Ibid.

8. Ibid.

9. Ibid.

10. Shirley Chisholm, *Unbought and Unbossed* (Washington, DC: Take Root Media, 1970), 91.

11. Luchina Fisher, "African American Women's Vote Key in 2001," *Women's Enews*, http://www.womensenews.org/story/campaign-trail/040329/african-ameri can-womens-vote-key-2004, accessed January 3, 2008.

12. Ibid.

13. Ibid.

14. Ibid.

15. Ibid.

16. "Pennsylvania Voters Elect Few Women, Blacks," MSNBC.com, http:// www.msnbc.msn.com/id/23883824/ns/politics-decision_08/t/pennsylvania-voters- elect-few-women-blacks/, accessed April 20, 2012.

17. Ibid.

18. Ibid.

19. Roslyn Terborg-Penn, *African American Women in the Struggle for the Vote, 1850–1920* (Bloomington: Indiana University Press, 1998), 65.

20. Ibid.

21. *The Challenges of Race and Gender,* The National Organization for African American Women, survey, 2009.

22. Boyce Watkins, "Black Female Voters Not Getting the Respect That They Deserve," http://www.bvonmoney.com/2010/11/17/black-female-voting-block-not-receiving-the-respect-it-deserves/, accessed November 17, 2010.

23. "African Americans Vote Key in 2004," *Women's Enews,* http://www.women senews.org/story/campaign-trail/040329/african-americans-vote-key-2004, accessed January 3, 2008.

24. David Bositis, *The Black Vote in 2004,* Joint Center for Political and Economic Studies, January 1, 2005.

25. Ibid.

26. "Kerry and Women, Too Little, Too Late," *Women's Enews,* http://www.women senews.org/story/campaign-trail/041106/kerry-and-women-too-little-too-late, accessed January 3, 2008.

27. Bositis, *The Black Vote in 2004.*

28. "Kerry and Women, Too Little, Too Late."

29. Ibid.

30. Bositis, *The Black Vote in 2004.*

31. U.S. Department of Education, www.ed.gov, accessed June 2, 2010.

32. Centers for Disease Control, "HIV among African Americans," 2011, http://www.cdc.gov/hiv/topics/aa/pdf/aa.pdf, accessed May 30, 2011.

Chapter 2 A Look Back

1. Peter J. Ling and Sharon Monteith, *Gender and the Civil Rights Movement* (Piscataway, NJ: Rutgers University Press, 2004).

2. Rachel L. Swarns, "Quiet Political Shifts as More Blacks are Elected," *New York Times,* October 13, 2008. http://www.nytimes.com/2008/10/14/us/po litics/14race.html, accessed May 4, 2012.

3. "Black History Fact of the Week: Shirley Chisholm," *Our Weekly,* http://www.ourweekly.com/los-angeles/black-history-fact-week-shirley-chisholm, accessed January 31, 2011.

4. Susan J. Carroll and Krista Jenkins, "Unrealized Opportunity? Term Limits and the Representation of Women in State Legislature," *Center for American Women in Politics* http://www.capwip.org/readingroom/termlimits_unrealized.PDF.

5. "Presidential Campaign Finance," http://www.gwu.edu/~action/2008/pres fin08.html, accessed May 4, 2012.

6. National Organization of African American Women Survey, 2009 http://freeonlinesurveys.com/v1/rendersurvey.asp?sid=0d2nz36lgzvtaau522000.

Chapter 3 Racial Bias within the Women's Suffrage Movement

1. "Women of Achievement, Abigail Adams," Herbert Hoover Presidential Library and Exhibits, http://www.hoover.archives.gov/exhibits/AmericanWomen/colony-country/adams.html, accessed July 17, 2011.

2. Ibid.

3. "Seneca Falls Convention, July 19–20, 1848," The National Portrait Gallery, http://npg.si.edu/col/seneca/senfalls1.htm, accessed May 7, 2012.

4. Donna L. Franklin, *What's Love Got to Do with It?* (New York: Simon & Schuster, 2000), 150.

5. "Life After the 13th Amendment," http://www.history.rochester.edu/class/douglass/part5.html, accessed July 1, 2001.

6. Leith Mullings, *On Our Own Terms: Race, Class, and Gender in the Lives of African American Women* (New York: Routledge, 1997), 45.

7. Deborah G. White, *Too Heavy a Load: Black Women in Defense of Themselves, 1894–1994* (New York: WW. Norton, 1999), 45.

8. Ibid.

9. "Women Marchers Attacked at Inauguration," http://womenshistory.about.com/library/weekly/aa010118b, accessed May 7, 2012.

10. Franklin, *What's Love Got to Do with It?*, 48.

11. Ellen Carol DuBois and Richard Candida Smith, *Elizabeth Cady Stanton, Feminist as Thinker: A Reader in Documents and Essays* (New York: New York University Press, 2007), 197.

Chapter 4 Gender Bias within the Civil Rights Movement

1. "The March on Washington for Jobs and Freedom," http://www.crmvet.org/info/mow.pdf, accessed May 14, 2012.

2. Vicki Crawford, Jacqueline Anne Rouse, and Barbara Woods, *Women in the Civil Rights Movement* (Bloomington: Indiana University Press, 1990).

3. Ibid., 94.

4. "History Is a Weapon: The Montgomery Bus Boycott," http://www.history isaweapon.com/defcon1/wpcmontgomery.html, accessed May 7, 2012.

5. Darlene Clark Hine, *Black Women in America: An Historical Encyclopedia* (New York: Carlson Publishing, 1993).

6. Cynthia Stokes Brown, *Ready from Within: Septima Clark and the Civil Rights Movement* (Navarro, CA: Wild Trees Press, 1986), 79.

7. Paula Giddings, *When and Where I Enter: The Impact of Black Women on Race and Sex in America* (New York: W. Morrow, 1984), 284.

8. Yussuf Simmonds, "Fannie Lou Hamer," *Los Angeles Sentinel*, October 2, 2008.

9. Crawford, Rouse, and Woods, *Women in the Civil Rights Movement,* 94.

10. "Septima Clark: Teacher to a Movement," unpublished article by J. Douglas Allen-Taylor, http://www.safero.org/articles/septima.html, accessed July 17, 2011.

11. Ibid.

12. Ibid.

13. Ibid.

14. Stokes Brown, *Ready from Within,* 79.

15. "An Agent of Change: Septima Poinsette Clark," Archives and Research Library of the Charles H. Wright Museum of African American History, http://chwmaah-archive.com/?p=3460, accessed July 11, 2011.

16. Giddings, *When and Where I Enter,* 284.

17. Crawford, Rouse, and Woods, *Women in the Civil Rights Movement,* 94.

18. "All Woman: Amy Jacques Garvey," http://www.unia-acl.com/Amy%20Jacques/Amy%20Euphemia%20Jacques%20Garvey%20Bio.pdf.

19. Ibid.

20. Zita Allen, *Black Women Leaders of the Civil Rights Movement* (Danbury, CT: Franklin Watts, 1996).

21. Devon Carbado, *Black Men on Race, Gender, and Sexuality* (New York: New York University Press, 1999).

Chapter 5 The Shortcomings of Black Feminism

1. Patricia Hill Collins, *Black Feminist Thought* (New York: Rutledge, 1990), 20.

2. Ibid.

3. Ibid.

4. Mary Ann Weathers, "An Argument for Black Women's Liberation as a Revolutionary Force," *No More Fun and Games: A Journal of Female Liberation* 1 (February 1969): 2, http://scriptorium.lib.duke.edu.wim/fun-games2/, accessed July 1, 2011.

5. Combahee River Collective, "A Black Feminist Statement," in *Capitalist Patriarchy and the Case for Socialist Feminism,* ed. Zillah Eisenstein (New York: Monthly Review Press, 1979).

6. Ibid.

7. Collins, *Black Feminist Thought,* 222.

8. Ibid., 6.

9. Ibid., 7.

10. Ibid., 33.

Chapter 6 The 2008 Presidential Election: Substance or Symbolism?

1. New York Women in Communications Commissioned Survey, 2007, http://www.reuters.com/article/2008/01/02/idUS153385+02-Jan-2008+BW20080102, accessed May 14, 2012.

2. Rasmussen Reports, http://www.rasmussenreports.com/public_content/pol itics/political_updates/president_bush_job_approval accessed January 5, 2010.

3. Lisa Chedekel and Regine Laboissiere, "The Dilemma of Gender and Race: Voters Weigh Implications of Unprecedented Choice," *Hartford Courant,* January 27, 2008.

4. Super Tuesday; Democratic Races, http://politics.nytimes.com/election-guide/2008/supertuesday/democraticpreview/, accessed May 14, 2012.

5. Perry Bacon Jr., "Can Obama Count on the Black Vote?" *Time,* http://www.time.com/time/nation/article/0%2C8599%2C1581666%2C00.html, accessed February 10, 2009.

6. "African American Politics and Welfare," http://www.neoperspectives.com/blackconservatism.html, accessed January 2008.

7. Eli Saslow, "To Women, So Much More than Just a Candidate," *Washington Post,* March 4, 2008.

8. South Carolina Election Center 2008, CNN Politics.com, www.cnn.com/ELECTION/2008/states/south.carolina.html, accessed September 2008.

9. Michelle Peltier, "Black Women Prefer Clinton to Obama," CBSnews.com, http://www.cbsnews.com/stories/2007/12/02/politics/main3562837.shtml, accessed April 2008.

10. Celinda Lake and Joshua Ulibarri, *The Rising American Electorate,* Lake Research Partners, December 6, 2011. http://www.lakeresearch.com/news/RAE/SHORT_RAE_subset.pdf, accessed May 14, 2012.

11. Kristin Ketteringham, "Single Parent Households—How Does It Affect the Children?" *Lifestyle,* July 6, 2007.

12. Froma Harrop, "Single Women Emerging as Key Presidential Voting Bloc," *HeraldNet,* January 30, 2008.

13. Lake and Ulibarri, *The Rising American Electorate.*

14. Ibid.

15. Ibid.

16. Ibid.

17. David A. Bositis, personal interview with author October 28, 2010.

18. Marcia Wade, "Black Women a Key Vote in Election 2004?" *Black Enterprise Magazine,* August 2004.

19. Data are from U.S. Census Bureau, Current Population Survey Voting and Registration in the Election of November 2004, Issued March 2006, http://www.census.gov/prod/2006pubs/p20-556.pdf.

20. "Election 2004," CNN.com, http://www.cnn.com/ELECTION/2004, accessed April 2010.

21. Ibid.

22. David Bositis, "The Black Vote in 2004," Joint Center for Political and Economic Studies, January 1, 2005.

23. Ibid.

24. Ibid.

25. Lake and Ulibarri, *The Rising American Electorate*.

Chapter 7 Early Indicators of Gender Preference Shift to Racial Preference

1. *The Challenges of Choosing Between Race and Gender*, National Organization for African American Women survey, 2008.

2. Ibid.

3. "Poll: Black Support Helps Clinton Extend Lead," CNN, http://articles.cnn.com/2007–10–17/politics/poll.blacks.democrats_1_black-voters-african-american-voters-black-women?_s=PM:POLITICS, accessed September 17, 2009.

4. Ibid.

5. CBS News/*New York Times* Poll, "Hillary Clinton, Women Voters and the 2008 Election," July 9–17, 2007.

6. Ibid.

7. Ibid.

8. U.S. Census Bureau, Key Facts On Census Income And Poverty Report, September 30, 1999, http://clinton4.nara.gov/WH/EOP/nec/html/FurmanCensus990930.html, accessed August 1, 2010.

9. Voter News Service exit poll, reported in the *New York Times*, November 10, 1996, p. 28.

10. "The Clinton Presidency: Historic Economic Growth," New Democrat Network (NDN), April 25, 2005.

11. "The Clinton Gore Administration: A Record of Progress," http://clinton4.nara.gov/WH/Accomplishments/african-long.html, accessed April 14, 2011.

12. CBS News/*New York Times* Poll, "Hillary Clinton."

13. "Female Candidates Face Pressure from Female Voters," USAToday.com, http://www.usatoday.com/news/politics/2007-05-01-women-candidates_N.html, accessed May 14, 2012.

14. Michael McAuliffe, *New York Daily News*, July 18, 2007.

15. CBS News/*New York Times* Poll, "Hillary Clinton."

16. Ibid.

Chapter 8 The Consequential Shift to Obama

1. David Bernstein. "The Speech," *Chicago Magazine*, June 2007.

2. Ibid.

3. Emily Cadei, "Obama Outshines Other Candidates in January Fundraising," *CQ Politics*, February 21, 2008.

4. Jim Malone, "Obama Fundraising Suggests Close Race for Party Nomination," *Voice of America*, July 2, 2007.

5. Jeanne Cummings, "Small Donors Rewrite Fundraising Handbook," *Politico*, September 26, 2007.

6. *The Challenges of Choosing Between Race and Gender*, National Organization for African American Women Survey, 2009.

7. Tony Norman, "Gov. 'Blunt Talk' Rendell," *Pittsburgh Post-Gazette*, February 12, 2008.

8. "US Moves a Step Forward with Obama," http://www.snnbd.com/mnews-n.php?id=9884&cid=0.02, accessed March 21, 2010.

9. Allison Hoffman, "Oprah Winfrey Holds Fundraiser for Obama," Associated Press, September 8, 2007.

10. "The Missing Oprah Bounce," http://voices.washingtonpost.com/44/2007/12/11/the_missing_oprah_bounce.html, accessed March 10, 2010.

11. *The Challenges of Choosing Between Race and Gender.*

12. "Obama Draws Comparisons to MLK. JFK," http://www.norwichbulletin.com/x603843185#axzz1mE1vgEXO, accessed March 21, 2010.

13. "Poll: Obama Makes Big Gains among Black Voters," CNN, http://articles.cnn.com/2008-01-18/politics/poll.2008_1_obama-new-poll-clinton-stronghold?_s=PM:POLITICS, accessed July 20, 2011.

14. Mark Blumenthal, "The 2008 Race," http://www.pollster.com/blogs/the_2008_race/, accessed March 21, 2010.

15. "New Poll: US More Ready for Black Prez than Female One," http://latimesblogs.latimes.com/washington/2008/01/blacks.html, 2008, accessed March 21, 2010.

16. Ibid.

17. Michael Saul, "Barack Obama Claims Historic Win," NYDailyNews.com, June 3, 2008, http://articles.nydailynews.com/2008-06-03/news/17898987_1_hillary-clinton-barack-obama-john-mccain, accessed March 21, 2010.

Chapter 9 The Historic 2008 Democratic Primaries and Caucuses

1. Presidential Primary, http://www.rtbot.net/presidential_primary, accessed May 12, 2012 .

2. Fredreka Schouten, "Democrats Hold Cash Edge over Republicans in '08 Bids," *USA Today*, October 16, 2007.

3. The New Hampshire Department of State Web site, http://www.sos.nh.gov/presprim2008/FILE%20FOR%20PRESIDENTIAL%20PRIMARY.pdf, accessed March 17, 2010.

4. Adele Stan, "Can Black Women Save the Democratic Coalition?" *The American Prospect*, January 25, 2008.

5. "Analysis: Bill Clinton's Lost Legacy," CBS News, June 18, 2009.

6. Real Clear Politics, "2008 Democratic Popular Vote," http://www.realclearpolitics.com/epolls/2008/president/democratic_vote_count.html, accessed May 12, 2012.

7. David Mark and David Paul Kuhn, "Clinton Tops Obama among African Americans," *Politico*, www.politico.com, accessed November 27, 2007.

8. Mark and Kuhn, "Clinton Tops Obama."

9. Mark Mooney, "Bubba: Obama is Just Like Jesse Jackson," ABC News, January 26, 2008.

10. Nitya, "Obama Raises Record $32 Million in January," ABC News, January 31, 2008, http://abcnews.go.com/blogs/politics/2008/01/obama-raises-32-2/, accessed June 11, 2011.

11. Patrick Healy and Jeff Zeleny, "Obama Outshines Clinton at Raising Funds," *New York Times*, February 8, 2008.

12. Ibid.

13. Kent Garber, "High Democratic Turnout Sends a Mixed Signal for November," *U.S. News & World Report*, February 28, 2008.

14. Justin M. Sizemore, "How Obama Did It: Big States, Small States, Caucuses and Campaign Strategy," Center for Politics, June 5, 2008.

15. Ibid.

16. Leslie Wayne, "Democratic Donations Keep Pouring In, but for Clinton, There's a Catch," *New York Times*, March 22, 2008.

17. Sizemore, "How Obama Did It: Big States."

18. Ibid.

19. Ibid.

20. Ibid.

21. Ibid.

Chapter 10 An Influential New Voting Bloc Emerges

1. "Profile of the Pennsylvania Primary Voters," *The New York Times*, April 2008.

2. Jennifer Parker, "Democratic Women Torn Between Clinton and Obama," ABC News, February 4, 2008.

3. "Hillary Clinton More Popular among Black Women than Obama," *The Indiana Express*, December 5, 2007, http://www.indianexpress.com/news/hillary-more-popular-among-black-women-than-obama/246743, accessed May 14, 2012.

4. Mark, Leibovich, "Welcome Back Clinton," *New York Times*, June 24, 2008.

5. Adam Nagourney, "Obama Wins Election," *New York Times*, November 4, 2008.

6. "Black Support Helps Clinton Extend Lead," CNN.com, October 17, 2007, http://edition.cnn.com/2007/POLITICS/10/17/poll.blacks.democrats/index.html, accessed May 14, 2012.

7. Sherrel Wheeler Stewart, "Election Survey: Women Care About Integrity, Leadership Ability More than Race, Gender," BlackAmericaWebb.com, April 25,

2008, http://www.spelman.edu/about_us/distinction/leads/pdf/BlackAmericaWeb Article_ElectionSurvey.pdf, accessed May 14, 2012.

8. Yvonne Scruggs-Leftwich, "Significance of Black Women's Vote Ignored," *Women's Enews*, Womensenews.com, November 15, 2010, http://womensenews. org/story/commentary/001115/significance-black-womens-vote-ignored, accessed May 23, 2010.

9. Ibid.

10. Voter Registration in the Election of 2004, U.S. Census Bureau statistics.

11. Ibid.

12. "The Office of Minority Health, U.S. Department of Health and Human Services," http://www.omhrc.gov, accessed May 23, 2010.

13. David Bositis, "The Black Vote in 2004," Joint Center for Political and Economic Studies, January 2005, http://www.jointcenter.org/sites/default/files/up load/research/files/BlackVote2004.pdf, accessed April 5, 2012.

14. Ibid.

15. Luchina Fisher, "African American Women's Vote Key in 2004," *Women's Enews*, Womensenews.org, March 29, 2004, http://womensenews.org/story/cam paign-trail/040329/african-american-womens-vote-key-2004, accessed May 12, 2012.

16. Ibid.

17. Ibid.

18. Kenneth Kim, "Did Asian Americans Swing California for Clinton?" *New America Media*, February 7, 2008, http://news.newamericamedia.org/news/view_ar ticle.html?article_id=d7a4a2a86575f4bfbc4e0e32a87a448d, accessed May 14, 2012.

19. Ibid.

20. Britta Waldschmidt-Nelson, "The Struggle Continues: Black Women in Congress in the 1990s," in *Gender and the Civil Rights Movement*, ed. Peter J. Ling and Sharon Monteith (New York: Rutgers University Press, 1999), 241.

21. Ibid.

Chapter 11 A Renewed Sense of Obligation

1. Rob Richie, "Ten Surprises about Election '08," HuffingtonPost.com, posted November 6, 2008, http://www.fairvote.org/ten-surprises-about-election-2008, ac cessed November 8, 2008.

2. "Women's Vote Clinches Election Victory: Gender Gap Large in Key Battle ground States Where African American Women Make Their Voices Heard," PR Newswire, November 6, 2008.

3. Britta Waldschmidt-Nelson, "The Struggle Continues," in *Gender and the Civil Rights Movement*, ed. Peter J. Ling and Sharon Monteith (New Brunswick, NJ: Rutgers University Press, 2004), 243.

4. Ibid.

5. Ibid.

6. "Census Report: Broad Racial Disparities Persist," http://www.msnbc.msn.com/id/15704759/ns/us_news-life, accessed July 20, 2011,

7. Lisa Nikol Nealy, "African American Women Voters," in *African American Women Voters: Racializing Religiosity, Political Consciousness and Progressive Political Action in U.S. Presidential Elections from 1964 through 2008* (Lanham, MD: University Press of America, 2009), 94.

8. Ibid.

9. Paula Giddings, *When and Where I Enter: The Impact of Black Women on Race and Sex in America* (New York: W. Morrow, 1984), 349.

10. Adele Stan, "Can Black Women Save the Liberal Coalition?" *The American Prospect*, January 25, 2008, http://prospect.org/article/can-black-women-save-liberal-coalition, accessed January 26, 2008.

11. Waldschmidt-Nelson, "The Struggle Continues," 251.

12. Susan J. Carroll, *Women and American Politics: New Questions, New Directions* (New York: Oxford University Press).

Chapter 12 The Fulfillment of the Thirteenth and Nineteenth Amendments

1. "Dissecting the 2008 Electorate: Most Diverse in U.S. History," Pew Research Center, http://pewresearch.org/assets/pdf/dissecting-2008-electorate.pdf, accessed January 30, 2010.

2. Ibid.

3. Darrell M. West, "Hillary and Obama: Is America Ready for a Non-White or Female President?" http://www.insidepolitics.org/heard/WestReport207.html, accessed July 8, 2011.

4. Eric Stirgus, "Atlanta's Black Women Voters in Play," *Atlanta Journal Constitution*, October 4, 2009.

5. Britta Waldschmidt-Nelson, "The Struggle Continues: Black Women in Congress in the 1990s," in *Gender and the Civil Rights Movement*, ed. Peter J. Ling and Sharon Monteith (New York: Rutgers University Press, 1999).

6. Ibid.

7. The Office of Minority Health, U.S. Department of Health and Human Services, http://www.omhrc.gov, accessed May 25, 2010.

8. Ibid.

9. Ibid.

10. Susan J. Carroll, *Women and American Politics: New Questions, New Directions* (New York: Oxford University Press, 2003), 203.

11. Gallop Poll News Service, www.cawp.rutgers.edu/Facts/Elections/pres08_polls/Gallup_6in10.pdf, accessed August 2, 2010.

12. Carroll, *Women and American Politics,* 196.

13. Ibid.

14. Democracynow.org [video presentation], http://www.democracynow.org/
2008/1/14/race_and_gender_in_presidential_politics, accessed August 4, 2011.

15. Courtesy of The Commonwealth Club of California, May 7, 2008, San
Francisco, California.

16. Aaron Blake, "Independent Voters Big for GOP; Democrats Maintain Black
Vote," *The Hill,* November 4, 2009.

17. Dr. Philip J. Ardoin and Dr. Ronald J. Vogel, "African Americans and the
Republican Party: Taking the Road Less Travelled," research paper, Appalachian
State University, http://www.appstate.edu/~ardoinpj/research/African%20Ameri
cans%20in%20the%20Republican%20Party.pdf, accessed May 14, 2012.

Chapter 13 The 2008 Presidential Election: The Choice

1. Mark Hugo Lopez and Paul Taylor, "Dissecting the 2008 Electorate, Most
Diverse in U.S. History," Pew Research Center, April 30, 2009.

2. *The Challenges of Choosing between Race and Gender,* National Organization for African American Women Survey, 2009.

3. Ibid.

4. Chris Suellentrop, "The Rep Who Cries Racism," Slate.com, http://www.
slate.com/articles/news_and_politics/assessment/2002/04/cynthia_mckinney.
html, accessed April 19, 2012.

5. Dayo Olopade, "Why Are There So Few Black Women Politicians?" *The
Root,* March 9, 2010.

6. Ibid., 339.

7. "Survey: Democratic Votes Drop in Strong States Scoop," *Independent
News,* November 11, 2009.

8. Karyn Strickler, "Reviving a Progressive Agenda in America by Achiev-
ing Gender Balance in Politics," DemocraticUnderground.com, April 29, 2005,
http://www.democraticunderground.com/articles/05/04/29_balance.html, accessed
March 25, 2010.

9. Martin Kilson, "Anatomy of Black Conservatism," *JSTOR: Transition* 59 (1993).

10. Chris McGreal, "U.S. Elections 2012: Tensions Over Race Likely to Suppress
Black Vote," *The Guardian,* January 18, 2012, http://www.guardian.co.uk/world/
2012/jan/18/south-carolina-primary-racial-tension, accessed May 14, 2012.

11. Ibid.

Conclusion

1. Dr. Jason Johnson, "What Barack Obama Owes African American Women,"
Tri-State Defender Online, February 9, 2012, http://tri-statedefenderonline.com/

articlelive/articles/7198/1/What-Barack-Obama-owes-African-American-women/Page1.html, accessed February 15, 2012.

2. Ibid.

3. Deborah White, "African American Population by State in 2010," About.com, http://usliberals.about.com/od/Election2012Factors/a/African-American-Population-By-State.html, accessed May 10, 2012.

4. Mark Hugo Lopez and Paul Taylor, "Dissecting the 2008 Electorate: Most Diverse in U.S. History," Pew Research Center, April 30, 2009.

5. Ibid.

6. Ibid.

7. Ibid.

8. Page Gardner, "Portrait of Unmarried African American Women and the Importance of Economic Issues in the 2008 Election," http://www.voterparticipation.org/wp-content/uploads/2011/09/afam_web.pdf, October 17, 2011.

9. Ibid.

10. Ibid.

11. Krissah Thompson and Vanessa Williams, "African American Women See Their Own Challenges Mirrored in Michelle Obama's," *Washington Post,* January 23, 2012.

12. Ibid.

13. "Hillary Clinton Endorses Barack Obama," transcript, August 26, 2008, http://elections.nytimes.com/2008/president/conventions/videos/transcripts/20080826_CLINTON_SPEECH.html, accessed February 1, 2012.

14. Gardner, "Portrait of Unmarried African American Women."

15. Ibid.

16. Center for American Women and Politics, "Facts on Women of Color in Elective Office," http://www.cawp.rutgers.edu/fast_facts/women_of_color/elective_office.php, accessed September 14, 2011.

17. Laurie K. Blandford, "Will Fort Pierce Voters Elect City's First Female or Black Mayor?" TCPALM.com, March 6, 2012, http://m.tcpalm.com/news/2012/mar/06/will-fort-pierce-voters-elect-citys-first-female, accessed March 15, 2012.

18. City-Data.com, "Fort Pierce, Florida," http://www.city-data.com/city/Fort-Pierce-Florida.html, accessed February 1, 2012.

Afterword

1. Virginia Leadership Institute, http://www.virginialead.org/background.html, accessed July 21, 2011.

2. David A. Bositis, "Blacks and the 2010 Midterms: A Preliminary Analysis," Joint Center for Political Economic Studies, November 16, 2010.

3. Ibid.

4. Ibid.

5. Courtland Milloy, "Adrian Fenty's Snubs of Black Women Make a Win at the Polls Unlikely," *The Washington Post,* August 25, 2010.

6. Paul Schwartzman and Chris L. Jenkins, "How DC Mayor Fenty Lost the Black Vote and His Job," *The Washington Post,* September 18, 2010.

7. The Gender and Multi-cultural Leadership Project, http://www.gmcl.org/pdf/GMCL_Executive_Summary.pdf, accessed December 8, 2010

8. Bositis, "Blacks and the 2010 Midterms."

9. Center for Women in American Politics, http://www.cawp.rutgers.edu, August 21, 2010.

10. "Roland Burris Says Goodbye to the Senate," CBS News, November 19, 2010.

11. The Gender and Multi-cultural Leadership Project.

12. Ibid.

Bibliography

Allen, Zita. *Black Women Leaders of the Civil Rights Movement.* Danbury, CT: Franklin Watts, 1996.

Carroll, Susan J. *Women and American Politics: New Questions, New Directions.* Oxford, UK: Oxford University Press, 2003.

Clark, Septima Poinsette, and Cynthia Stokes Brown. *Ready from Within: Septima Clark and the Civil Rights Movement.* Navarro, CA: Wild Trees Press, 1986.

Collins, Patricia. *Black Feminist Thought: Knowledge, Consciousness, and the Politics of Empowerment.* New York: Routledge, 2000.

Crawford, Vicky L., Jacqueline Anne Rouse, and Barbara Woods. *Women in the Civil Rights Movement.* Bloomington: Indiana University Press, 1993.

DuBois, Ellen Carol, and Richard Smith. *Elizabeth Cady Stanton, Feminist as Thinker: A Reader in Documents and Essays.* New York: New York University Press, 2007.

Franklin, Donna L. *What's Love Got to Do With It?: Understanding and Healing the Rift Between Black Men and Women.* New York: Simon & Schuster, 2000.

Giddings, Paula. *When and Where I Enter: The Impact of Black Women on Race and Sex in America.* New York: W. Morrow, 1984.

Guide to U.S. Elections. Washington, DC: CQ Press, 2010.

Hine, Darlene Clark, Elsa Barkley Brown, and Rosalyn Penn. *Black Women in America: An Historical Encyclopedia.* Brooklyn, NY: Carlson, 1993.

hooks, bell. *Ain't I a Woman: Black Women and Feminism.* Boston, MA: South End Press, 1999.

Hull, Gloria T., Patricia Scott, and Barbara Smith. *All the Women are White, All the Blacks Are Men, but Some of Us Are Brave: Black Women's Studies.* Old Westbury, NY: Feminist Press, 1982.

Ling, Peter J., and Sharon Monteith. *Gender and the Civil Rights Movement.* New Brunswick, NJ: Rutgers University Press, 2004.

Mullings, Leith. *On Our Own Terms: Race, Class, and Gender in the Lives of African American Women.* New York: Routledge, 1997.

Nealy, Lisa Nikol. *African American Women Voters: Racializing Religiosity, Political Consciousness and Progressive Political Action in U.S. Presidential Elections from 1964 through 2008.* Lanham, MD: University Press of America, 2009.

Palmer, Barbara, and Dennis Michael Simon. *Breaking the Political Glass Ceiling: Women and Congressional Elections.* New York: Routledge, 2006.

Smith, Jessie Carney. *Black Firsts: Ground-Breaking Events in African American History.* 2nd ed. Detroit: Visible Ink Press, 2009.

Terborg-Penn, Roslyn. *African American Women in the Struggle for the Vote, 1850–1920.* Bloomington: Indiana University Press, 1998.

White, Deborah G. *Too Heavy a Load: Black Women in Defense of Themselves, 1894–1994.* New York: W.W. Norton, 1999.

Index

About the Author

CINDY HOOPER is a veteran of numerous local, state, and national political campaigns. She has a master's degree in government from The Johns Hopkins University. She is the founder of the National Organization for African American Women, headquartered in Washington, DC.